FOR HELEN

In wildness is the preservation of the world.

HENRY DAVID THOREAU
Journal, Volume I

The Nature Journal

A Monthly Guide to Wildlife

Written by Miriam Anne Bourne
Illustrated by Marjorie Stodgell

Starwood Publishing, Inc.
Washington, D.C.

In memory of Miriam Anne Bourne and
her lifelong commitment to nature study,
a portion of the proceeds from the sales
of *The Nature Journal* will be contributed
to the National Wildlife Federation.

Illustrated by *Marjorie Stodgell*
Edited by *Gil Kline*
Designed by *Sicklesmith Design*
Permissions credited on page 108.
Text copyright © 1990 by *Miriam Anne Bourne*.
All rights reserved.
Copyright © 1990 by *Starwood Publishing, Inc.*
All rights reserved. No part of the contents
of this book may be reproduced without the
 written permission of the publisher.

ISBN 0-912347-39-2
Printed in Singapore by *Palace Press*

5 4 3 2 1   97 96 95 94 93 92 91 90

INTRODUCTION

The Nature Journal SHARES WITH THE READER THE SIGHTS AND sounds of our natural world as it changes with the turning of the seasons—that "Wonderful Rotation," as Emily Dickinson called it. The journal offers facts and impressions of North American wildlife over time and across habitats: in forest and meadow, pond and marsh, shore and sky. ❁ It is meant to encourage us to pause and look carefully and closely into the forest, where the woodland jumping mouse leaps over millipedes and hoary mountain mint, to look closer still at the pond, where the dragonfly and damselfly hover over water hyacinth and arrowhead, or in the meadow, where the ruby-throated hummingbird flits among columbines and buttercups. ❁ Organized month by month, the journal also includes separate sections on the plants and animals of special regions: the Everglades *(February),* Hawaii *(March),* the Prairies *(June),* the alpine and tundra regions *(July),* and the Pacific Coast *(December).* A checklist at the end of each month allows you to record your sightings, to add new ones, and to jot down observations. ❁ "Of all the wonderful things in the wonderful universe of God," wrote 19th-century gardener Celia Thaxter, "nothing seems to me more surprising than the planting of a seed in the blank earth and the result thereof." ❁ We have planted our own seedlings of poetry and sketches throughout this journal, along with remarks by venerable naturalists such as John James Audubon, Roger Tory Peterson, Cordelia Stanwood, Edwin Way Teale, and Henry David Thoreau. Thanks also must be given to the colorful observations of friends Pat Fowler and Mort Matthew. ❁ And finally, many delightful verses were plucked from the library of this author's grandfather, where we are reminded that our timeless meditations on nature can forever be rediscovered, and help us to forever rediscover ourselves.

Think of our life in Nature,—daily to be shown matters to come
Into contact with it,—rocks, trees, wind on our cheeks! the
solid earth! The actual world! The common sense! Contact.
*Contact! Who are **we**? Who are **we**?*

HENRY DAVID THOREAU
"Ktaadn and the mountain woods"

—

January

At once a voice arose among
The bleak twigs overhead
In a full-hearted evensong
Of joy illimited;
An aged thrush, frail, gaunt, and small,
In blast-beruffled plume,
Had chosen thus to fling his soul
Upon the growing gloom.

THOMAS HARDY
"The Darkling Thrush"

January

The imaginative gardener sows his borders not only with red, pink and yellow hollyhocks, but also with red cardinals, rosy purple finches, and yellow grosbeaks.

ROGER TORY PETERSON

Gardening With Wildlife

BIRDS AT THE FEEDER

With a buzzy kind of winter call, **chicka-dees** sing "chick-a-dee-dee-dee," and "tseet, tseet." Grabbing a seed, they fly to a safe place and hold the seed with their feet, attacking it with a stubby bill. Accomplished acrobats, chickadees can feed upside down as they cling to tree branches.

chickadee

Peterson's *Field Guide to the Birds* describes the call of **juncos** as "a loose, quivering trill," a "musical tinkling," says the Audubon Society's *Encyclopedia*. These "snow birds" arrive in October from northern breeding grounds, probably returning to favorite foraging places, and hop along the ground seeking seeds fallen from feeders. A junco perched at the feeder may flash its white tail feathers to keep another in line.

Nuthatches can swoop from a tree headfirst, thanks to sharp claws on a toe at the rear of their feet, and they seldom come to the ground. They wedge a seed from the feeder into tree bark and crack it open with their sharp bills. **Brown-headed nuthatches** in the Southeast sometimes use a "tool" to feed. With a piece of bark in their bills, they chip at a tree to uncover insects.

"Yank, yank, yank," calls the **white-breasted nuthatch** in a low, nasal voice. Pairs stay within calling distance throughout the year. The **red-breasted**'s call is a higher "ank, ank, ank,"—a "tin whistle" to some ears. Nuthatches are partial to conifer seeds and migrate south in large numbers

January

when crops fail.

Blue jays screech at hawks and owls and mimic a wide variety of calls, but also possess their own sweet, musical song. As curious as their crow cousins and almost as raucous, jays migrate in flocks of fifty to one hundred. While they frequent oaks, they also will come to the feeder. Blue jays often eat gypsy moths, but their favorite delicacies are acorns and beechnuts which they store in the ground (nuts buried and misplaced become saplings).

You can tell it's a finch flying to the feeder by the undulations of its flight pattern—not the swoop of the jay nor the dart of the chickadee. Their dull green and yellow winter attire makes male **goldfinches** seem smaller than in the bright yellow of summertime. Goldfinches and **purple finches** flock to the thistle seed feeder and also eat weed seeds and maple and birch buds.

Below the feeder, corn and millet attract **mourning doves** unless there is crusty snow or they've migrated to dry uplands or other bare ground. When aloft, doves fly fast and their wings whistle.

Cardinals are proficient whistlers, with a repertory of some twenty-eight songs. The males sing in midwinter, while the females reply later in the season in a softer voice, much like their coloration. When cardinals pair off to mate, the flock breaks up.

The saucy **tufted titmice**, says Audubon, communicate in a "harsh, peevish" chatter, whistling over and over again, "Peter, Peter." In February titmice separate from the mixed, winter flocks to mate. Once paired, tufted titmice remain together for life and become more sedentary, staying near the nest throughout the year.

blue jay

January

In the Trees—Woodpeckers

Woodpeckers use resonate trees in the same way as other birds use song, says naturalist Donald Stokes in *A Guide to Nature in Winter*. Wielding sharp claws and tails for balance, woodpeckers hammer on trees to announce territory or to attract mates. Neck muscles drive their powerful bills, while their thick-walled skulls absorb the shock of the pounding. Woodpeckers also seek insects in trees. And while woodpeckers won't come to the bird feeder, they will to the suet.

Yellow-shafted flickers are the only woodpeckers in North America to feed from the ground (they're eating ants). **Hairy** and **downy woodpeckers** are look-alikes, except hairies are larger, their bills as long as their heads. Seeking wood-boring beetles for food, downies go to dead trees, hairies to live ones. The males of each have a red patch at the nape of the neck. When spring comes, it's the females who initiate courtship.

Red-headed woodpeckers are scarce in the Northeast and common in the South and Midwest. **Sapsuckers** make a ring of holes around a trunk, then devour the insects that come to drink the sap. The spectacular **pileated woodpeckers** are the largest, with a wingspread of twenty-seven to thirty inches (chickadees by comparison have a seven-to eight-inch span). Pileateds drill eight-inch holes hunting for carpenter ants.

Of the Fields and Marshes—the Sparrow

Most sparrows spend the cold months in the South. But **tree sparrows**—which have little to do with trees—summer just below the tundra and can survive low temperatures. In flocks of thirty to forty they feast on grass seeds in fields and marshes. Each has a large "stickpin" marking in the middle of its chest, and with its rusty cap is called a "winter chippy."

House sparrows, members of the weaverbird family, are famous for thriving in and around human habitats. They were introduced to the United

January

States from Europe in 1850—in Brooklyn, says one writer, in New York's Central Park, says another. Either way, they took to America.

You may talk for
all your days
In the thrush and bluebirds praise
And all your other harbingers of spring,
But I've never heard a song
Whose echoes I'd prolong
Like that I heard
that English sparrow sing

BERTHA JOHNSON
"Did You Ever Hear an
English Sparrow Sing?"

tree sparrow

KEEPING WARM

Birds have better resistance to cold than mammals and have higher body temperatures. Some grow extra insulating feathers in winter, tucking their feet and bills into them for warmth. Chickadees fluff out their feathers to trap air; when resting, they shiver to increase heat production. But all winter birds need shelter and plenty of high-glucose food to generate nourishment and warmth for those frozen nights.

"I thought it was your coat of feathers that kept you warm,"
said Peter [Rabbit to Tommy Tit, a chickadee].

"Oh, the feathers help," replied Tommy Tit. "Food makes heat
and a warm coat keeps the heat in the body. But the heat has got
to be there first, or the feathers will do no good. It's just the same
with your own self, Peter. You know you are never really warm

January

in winter unless you have plenty to eat....Why, sometimes in a single day I find and eat almost five hundred eggs of those little green plant lice that do so much damage in the spring and summer....Oh, there is plenty for me to do in the winter. I am one of the policemen of the trees. Downy and Hairy the Woodpeckers, Seep-Seep the Brown Creeper and Yank-Yank the Nuthatch are others. If we didn't stay right here on the job all winter, I don't know what would become of the Old Orchard."

THORNTON BURGESS

The Burgess Bird Book for Children

ROOSTING

At night flocks of birds sleep or rest together, usually at the same places in which they nest. Cardinals roost in thickets or join the blue jays, chickadees, grosbeaks, finches, and sparrows in evergreens. (The number of crows roosting in one place can reach an astonishing 200,000.) Songbirds have a way of "locking" their feet around a perch. They rest with head and neck on back, bill buried in shoulder. Woodpeckers hang onto the inside of a hole they've excavated in a tree, while nuthatches find snug holes, as do chickadees and brown creepers. Creepers also snooze in crevices in the bark.

CHECKLIST OF BIRDS SEEN

☐ blue jay; ☐ brown creeper; ☐ brown-headed nuthatch; ☐ cardinal; ☐ chickadee; ☐ crow; ☐ downy woodpecker; ☐ evening grosbeak; ☐ goldfinch; ☐ hairy wood-

evening grosbeaks

January

pecker; ☐ house sparrow; ☐ junco; ☐ mourning dove; ☐ pileated woodpecker; ☐ pine siskin; ☐ purple finch; ☐ red-breasted nuthatch; ☐ red-headed woodpecker; ☐ red poll; ☐ sapsucker woodpecker; ☐ tree sparrow; ☐ tufted titmouse; ☐ white-breasted nuthatch; ☐ yellow-shafted flicker.

☐ . . . .   ☐ . . . .   ☐ . . . .
☐ . . . .   ☐ . . . .   ☐ . . . .
☐ . . . .   ☐ . . . .   ☐ . . . .

PLANTS AND ANIMALS:

☐ . . . .   ☐ . . . .   ☐ . . . .
☐ . . . .   ☐ . . . .   ☐ . . . .
☐ . . . .   ☐ . . . .   ☐ . . . .
☐ . . . .   ☐ . . . .   ☐ . . . .
☐ . . . .   ☐ . . . .   ☐ . . . .

. . . .
. . . .
. . . .
. . . .
. . . .
. . . .
. . . .
. . . .
. . . .
. . . .
. . . .
. . . .
. . . .
. . . .

January

....
....
....
....
....
....
....
....
....
....
....
....
....
....
....
....
....
....
....
....
....
....
....
....
....
....
....
....
....
....
....
....

February

*For sounds in winter nights, and often
in winter days, I heard the forlorn but
melodious note of a hooting owl....
Sometimes I heard the foxes as they ranged
over the snow crust in moonlight nights,
in search of a partridge....Squirrels and
wild mice disputed for my store of nuts.*

HENRY DAVID THOREAU
Walden

February

ANIMALS IN WINTER

The night-hunting fox sniffs out rabbits and other game in field and forest. Mating takes place in January or February, after which double sets of tracks seen in the snow mean male and female are inspecting abandoned woodchuck holes in which to raise their family. The collie-sized **red fox** has black ears, nose, and lower legs and a white-tipped tail. The smaller **gray fox** is seen less frequently and climbs trees.

Celebrated for its affectionate family life, the **timber wolf** is the size of a large German shepherd but with longer legs. When hunting, it makes an elliptical circuit of established, marked routes, covering miles on a single night. Timber wolves are found throughout the forests of northern states. The smaller **coyote** (prairie wolf) carries its tail low when running and hunts in pairs or groups. Its famous howl is heard at night and early morning.

In winter, small herds of **white-tailed deer** feed in "deer yards," a concentrated network of trails, and bed together in places protected from the wind. The grass they eat in warm weather is now scarce, so they nibble evergreen needles, the few tree buds they can reach, and stay alert for hemlock tips dropped by porcupines chewing on them overhead.

Snowdrifts are a problem even for high-bounding, tail-flashing deer, but

white-tailed deer

16

February

in less deep snow they spread their cloven hoofs and can walk easier. Winter coats are a thick, brownish gray (summer coats are reddish brown). Bucks shed their antlers after the fall rutting season, a period of high sexual activity.

white-footed mouse

When angry or afraid, a rabbit stamps its hind feed; usually silent, it also can scream. The **cottontail rabbit** escapes from a red fox by hopping aside, doubling back, and inconspicuously "freezing" in place. Browsing on dry grasses, evergreen plants, and bark during the dusk, early morning, and moonlit nights, it stays close to cover and faces away from the wind. Winter is the only season when the cottontail does not mate. The **jack rabbit** and **varying hare** turn white in winter.

> *The mouse is a sober citizen who knows that grass grows in order that mice may store it as underground haystacks, and that snow falls in order that mice may build subways from stack to stack; supply, demand, and transport all neatly organized. To the mouse, snow means freedom from want and fear.*
>
> ALDO LEOPOLD
>
> *A Sand County Almanac*

The color of a summer deer on top and just as white below, the **white-footed mouse** has large eyes and ears and a long tail. Found in most woody or brushy places, this tiny creature climbs, leaps, gallops, and tunnels in the snow to reach caches of seeds and nuts. It taps with its feet, perhaps to announce territory, and makes a buzzing "song" and an occasional whistle.

To survive, the energetic **vole** (field mouse) has to eat its own weight every twenty-four hours. It forages under the snow for berries, roots, bulbs, and

seeds it has stored along long tunnels in marsh and meadow. Almost every animal and large bird seeks the vole for a meal, but nonstop production of litters (as many as seventeen a year) keeps voles thriving. Population explosions have wiped out entire crops and orchards.

The chipmunk-sized **weasel** has a handsome, ermine winter coat and a black-tipped tail. It has been called a "symbol of slaughter, sleeplessness, and tireless, incredible activity," according to the National Geographic Society in *Wild Animals of North America*. In the same family are the small **mink** and the elongated **otter**—both seen near the water—and the brown and orange **marten** and black **fisher**, two predators of the north woods. Their skunk-faced relative the **badger** lives in dry, open places and the bearlike **wolverine** is found only west of the Rockies.

A **bobcat** (wildcat) is about twice the size of a house cat, with short, white-tipped tail, "sideburns," and tufts of hair on its ears. The coats of those in northern forests are darker than those in the Southwest. A bobcat footprint shows no signs of the lethal claws because, like a domestic cat's, they can be retracted when not in use. They make their dens in rocky piles or under rocky ledges. Bobcats may rest in trees during the day and hunt primarily at night, on the ground, covering a twenty-five-mile territory marked with urine and scat.

A **Canada lynx**, the largest lynx in North America, also has a short tail but is larger than the bobcat. It lives only in the deep north woods and its chief food is the **snowshoe rabbit**. Its summer coat is red, with white below and spotted, and its winter coat is paler. The lynx grows hairs on its feet in winter for sure walking on the snow.

With a tawny coat and a long, droopy tail, the **mountain lion** (cougar or puma) is a much larger animal, weighing some 100 to 220 pounds. Its habitat ranges from icy mountain top to sweltering desert. This lion doesn't roar but can let out a chilling scream.

February

*We seem walking through an old-time woodcut, a study in black
and white. The snow-clad fields, the stark silhouettes of the trees
extend away from around us. Going down the lane and coming
back up the lane, we stop to gaze on the shadows of the hickory
trees lengthening over the drifts. All slant toward the west. But
they will swing in a slow half-circle as the frosty hours of the night
advance rotating in almost imperceptible movement over the snow
until, before dawn, they will slant toward the east. Recording the
passing of time by this slow sweep of their shadows, our hickories
beside the lane form the great moondial of our winter nights.*

EDWIN WAY TEALE

A Walk Through the Year

CHECKLIST

ANIMALS OR ANIMAL TRACKS:

☐ badger; ☐ bobcat; ☐ Canada lynx; ☐ cottontail rabbit; ☐ coyote;
☐ ferret; ☐ fisher; ☐ gray fox; ☐ marten; ☐ mink; ☐ mountain lion;
☐ otter; ☐ red fox; ☐ timber wolf; ☐ vole; ☐ weasel; ☐ white-footed
mouse; ☐ white-tailed deer.

☐ . . . .   ☐ . . . .   ☐ . . . .
☐ . . . .   ☐ . . . .   ☐ . . . .
☐ . . . .   ☐ . . . .   ☐ . . . .

BIRDS AND PLANTS:

☐ . . . .   ☐ . . . .   ☐ . . . .
☐ . . . .   ☐ . . . .   ☐ . . . .
☐ . . . .   ☐ . . . .   ☐ . . . .
☐ . . . .   ☐ . . . .   ☐ . . . .
☐ . . . .   ☐ . . . .   ☐ . . . .

February

EVERGLADES AND FLORIDA KEYS

PORTUGUESE MAN-O-WAR. A colorful jellyfish found on the surface of the ocean, the **Portuguese man-o'-war** has a sting almost as powerful as a cobra's venom. Its tentacles chemically paralyze crustaceans and small fish for capture. Strong winds can cast thousands of them on the shore, as sometimes happens in the Florida Keys. Most noticeable on the man-o'-war is its large, bladderlike, gas-filled float—up to a foot long and six inches wide and ranging in color from lavender to scarlet. In the ocean, the float when filled allows the wind to propel the jellyfish; when the man-o'-war wants to submerge, it deflates the float.

ANHINGA. Found throughout the Everglades, the **anhinga** (snakebird) swims with its body submerged, only neck and head above the water. By controlling the amount of air in its body, it can sink below for prey, using its serrated-edge bill, or rise above the surface. Its feathers are not waterproof like a duck's, so it must go to land to dry, where it often spreads its wings taking in the sun. Slow on land, it can spiral to great heights, soaring and making rapid clicking sounds. The anhinga has a small, snakelike head, fan-shaped tail, scarlet eyes, and silver on its forewings. The cormorant is very similar, but has a hook at the tip of its bill.

> *Here is in this river and in the waters all over Florida a very curious and handsome species of bird; the people call them snake birds [anhinga]. I think I have seen paintings of them on the Chinese screens and other India pictures. They seem to be a species of cormorant or loon, but far more beautiful and delicately formed than any other species that I have ever seen.*
>
> WILLIAM BARTRAM
> *John and William Bartram's America*

February

CHECKLIST—EVERGLADES AND FLORIDA KEYS

PLANTS:

☐ agave; ☐ airplants; ☐ brain and branch coral; ☐ cerith (horn shells); ☐ cockles; ☐ conch; ☐ cowries; ☐ cypress; ☐ gumbo-limbo; ☐ key lime tree; ☐ live oak; ☐ magnolia; ☐ mangrove; ☐ palmettos; ☐ royal palm; ☐ royal poinciana; ☐ saw grass; ☐ sea fans; ☐ Spanish moss; ☐ wild poinsettia.

☐ . . . .   ☐ . . . .   ☐ . . . .

☐ . . . .   ☐ . . . .   ☐ . . . .

☐ . . . .   ☐ . . . .   ☐ . . . .

ANIMALS AND BIRDS:

☐ alligator; ☐ anhinga; ☐ anole; ☐ brown pelican; ☐ chameleon; ☐ crocodile; ☐ Everglade kite; ☐ frigate bird; ☐ great blue heron; ☐ Gulf armadillo; ☐ key deer; ☐ limpkin; ☐ Portuguese man-o'-war; ☐ roseate spoonbill; ☐ skink; ☐ water moccasin; ☐ white ibis.

☐ . . . .   ☐ . . . .   ☐ . . . .

☐ . . . .   ☐ . . . .   ☐ . . . .

☐ . . . .

. . . .

. . . .

. . . .

. . . .

. . . .

. . . .

. . . .

. . . .

. . . .

. . . .

. . . .

alligator

February

March

The Pleiades their influence
now give
And all that seemed as dead
afresh doth live:
The croaking frogs, whom
nipping winter killed,
Like birds now chirp and hop
about the field.

ANNE BRADSTREET
"The Four Seasons of the Year"

March

It was evening all afternoon
It was snowing
And it was going to snow
The blackbird sat
In the cedar-limbs.

Wallace Stevens

"Thirteen Ways of Looking at a Blackbird"

Harmonium

One more snowstorm always comes in March—even in April. The first **robin** and the first **red-winged blackbird** often look as if they should have stayed South. But the snow won't last, and the early spring birds are here to stay: **fox sparrow**, **bluebird**, **mockingbird** (as far north as New England now), **Canada goose**, and **phoebe**.

Then from neighboring thicket the mocking bird,
wildest of singers,
Swinging aloft on a willow spray that hung
o'er the water,
Shook from his little throat such floods of
delirious music,
That the whole air and the woods and the
waves seemed silent to listen.

Henry Wadsworth Longfellow

"Evangeline"

At the feeder, the **evening grosbeak**'s bill is greener and soon the male **goldfinch** will grow his yellow courtship feathers. The **cardinal** and **tufted titmouse** are whistling.

March

MORE SIGNS OF SPRING

When the ground was partially bare of snow, and a few warm days had dried its surface somewhat, it was pleasant to compare the first tender signs of the infant year just peeping forth with the stately beauty of the withered vegetation which had withstood the winter—life-everlasting, goldenrods, pinweeds, and graceful wild grasses, more obvious and interesting frequently than in summer even, as if their beauty was not ripe till then; even cotton-grass, cat-tails, mulleins, johnswort, hardback, meadowsweet, and other strong-stemmed plants, those unexhausted granaries which entertain the earliest birds—decent weeds, at least, which widowed nature wears.

HENRY DAVID THOREAU
Walden

fox sparrow

On warm nights comes the rising trill of the **wood frog** calling for a mate, getting an early jump even on the persistent **spring peeper**. If it's rainy, you might see a brown, black-masked female peeper crossing the road toward a pond. She'll lay her eggs, then return to the woods. Daytimes, a few **wasps** and **spiders** are about, as are the lovely, early butterflies—the **spring azure** and **mourning cloak**.

Sap is running in the **maple trees** (**black birch** also has a sweet sap with an evergreen flavor). Finally gone are the pale leaves that clung to small **beech trees** much of the winter. Buds now are fatter; **willow** branches are yellow-green. **Catkins** appear on the **pussy willows** found in damp places, while the first **dandelions** and **chickweed** are blooming in the grass. Hunt for

March

hepatica and **trailing arbutus** in the woods. **Pondweeds** and **algae** are growing in still water; near fast-moving streams tightly curled fiddle-heads rise up along with **false hellebore** (Indian poke) and the purple spathe which surrounds the flowers of the **skunk cabbage**.

dandelions

NATURE'S ENGINEER

The best time to see a **beaver** is in the evening as its work begins. At this time of year the older of the two litters that spend the winter in the family "lodge" are leaving to construct new ones for themselves and to start their own families. A beaver constructs a dam to ensure that there will be deep enough water for food storage and for protection from larger animals. (Predators can cross the ice in winter, but frozen mud makes lodge walls impenetrable.)

Gnawed chips around a fallen tree stump that is pointed in the center are signs of a beaver's activity. Branches are chewed off in sizes that can be carried by mouth; logs are pushed over the ground and floated in specially dug canals to the building site. The beaver piles the wood—**poplar** and **aspen** are the preferred building materials—parallel to the current.

The lodge has two underwater entrances and a vent hole in the domed roof; a feeding platform and a sleeping floor are above water level. Bark is used to line the floor and, if necessary, for food. A winter supply of edible saplings will be stored underneath an entrance and anchored with stones or mud. Mud also is used to plug holes in the lodge or dam.

The beaver can stay submerged for as long as fifteen minutes, thanks to incredible attributes: extra-large lungs, livers full of oxygenated blood, an unusual tolerance for carbon dioxide, and valves that shut out water from nose

March

and ears. Oil glands under the tail waterproof the beaver's handsome, chestnut coat. The front feet are folded on the chest when swimming or used for carrying mud and stones; the strong hind feet are webbed. The beaver's paddle-shaped tail serves as a rudder, a warning device, and on land as a prop.

Beavers mate in January or February and stay together for life. About the time the yearlings depart, their father also leaves for a while; beavers often have a second home: a burrow in a bank by the stream. He'll return in a few weeks after the new kits are born to repair the lodge and make sure there's enough stored food.

Checklist

EARLY BIRDS:

☐ bluebird; ☐ Canada goose; ☐ cardinal; ☐ evening grosbeak; ☐ fox sparrow; ☐ goldfinch; ☐ mockingbird; ☐ phoebe; ☐ red-winged blackbird; ☐ robin; ☐ tufted titmouse.

☐ . . . . ☐ . . . .
☐ . . . . ☐ . . . .
☐ . . . . ☐ . . . .
☐ . . . . ☐ . . . .
☐ . . . . ☐ . . . .

tufted titmouse

OTHER WILDLIFE:

☐ butterfly; ☐ beaver; ☐ spider; ☐ spring peeper; ☐ wasp; ☐ wood frog.

☐ . . . . ☐ . . . . ☐ . . . .
☐ . . . . ☐ . . . . ☐ . . . .
☐ . . . . ☐ . . . . ☐ . . . .
☐ . . . . ☐ . . . . ☐ . . . .
☐ . . . . ☐ . . . . ☐ . . . .
☐ . . . . ☐ . . . . ☐ . . . .

March

PLANT LIFE:

☐ aspen; ☐ beech; ☐ black birch; ☐ catkin; ☐ chickweed; ☐ dandelion;
☐ false hellebore; ☐ hepatica; ☐ maple; ☐ mourning cloak; ☐ pond-
weed; ☐ pussy willow; ☐ skunk cabbage; ☐ spring azure; ☐ willow.

☐ . . . . ☐ . . . . ☐ . . . .

☐ . . . . ☐ . . . . ☐ . . . .

☐ . . . . ☐ . . . . ☐ . . . .

. . . .

. . . .

. . . .

. . . .

. . . .

. . . .

. . . .

. . . .

. . . .

. . . .

. . . .

. . . .

hepatica

March

HAWAII

At one time all wildlife arrived by bird
or by sea to these volcanic islands.
Insects and land snails are indige-
nous to the Hawaiian Islands, but
aside from the bat, land mammals were
later introduced by man. The mongoose

hibiscus

was brought in to kill rats in the 19th
century; it also exterminated two dozen bird species. More than twenty-
seven more bird species now are endangered, including the **nene goose**, the
state bird, for a variety of reasons.

Observe in these volcanic islands the curve-billed **honeycreeper**, the
green and yellow **anakihi** or the **elepaio**, a brown flycatcher. "Most native
Hawaiian birds are very shy and difficult to find," writes Sherwin Carlquist
in the Smithsonian's *American Land*. "The elepaio finds you."

On low, leeward mountain slopes you can find the **halo**, a common native
tree. Partway up the mountain in the dry forest zone is the state tree, the
kukui (candlenut). The **lehua**, which grows on higher, more humid slopes,
has showy red flowers.

Kauai, "the garden isle," is probably the best place to find bird and plant
life. Look for red and yellow **hibiscus** (5,000 varieties), yellow **ginger**, pink
and white **plumeria**, violet **jacaranda**, and scarlet **poinsettia** and **bou-
gainvillaea**, which you will find in leis as well as in gardens and the wild.
Orchids and **proteus** grow on the slopes of Mauna Loa Crater on Hawaii
and Haleakala Crater on Maui.

The distinctive and rare **silversword** is native and found only at
Haleakala. Once in a lifetime a gigantic cone covered with hundreds of
maroon flowers rises from these spectacular, glowing silver leaves and then
dies, leaving many seedlings to spring up around it.

March

. . . .
. . . .
. . . .
. . . .
. . . .
. . . .
. . . .
. . . .
. . . .
. . . .
. . . .
. . . .
. . . .
. . . .
. . . .
. . . .
. . . .
. . . .
. . . .
. . . .
. . . .
. . . .
. . . .
. . . .
. . . .
. . . .
. . . .

April

A fine morning. A Charming warm Day. Everything looks gay and lively. The Grass begins to spring, and the sprightly sunbeams gleam upon the houses. The windows are opened, the insects begin to buzz, and every thing welcomes the Joyful Spring.

JOHN ADAMS, *Diary Entry*

April

A mist of smoke, a mist of fog,
a mist of willow and alder catkins,
a mist of twigs and softly bursting buds,
a mist of shadbush and hobble bush blossoms,
and a mist of pine, fir, and spruce branches—
    that is today!

CORDELIA STANWOOD

Beyond The Spring by Chandler S. Richmond

Warmer, longer days bring **bees** to bulb, shrub, and tree blossoms. **Fish** and **tadpoles** swim in the brook. **Turtles** and **snakes** sun on the warm rocks, and fiddleheads are turning to **ferns** along the water's edge. April showers turn grass green. In the woods **moss** shines with an emerald color and new tips of **evergreens** are lighter than the rest. One final, unexpected snowstorm may fall, making the fresh greens even brighter still against the white; lingering **partridge berries** glisten a brilliant red.

The warmth of yesterday and this day forwarded vegetation very much; the buds of some trees, particularly the weeping willow and maple, had displayed their leaves and blossoms, and all others were swelled and many ready to put forth.

GEORGE WASHINGTON

Diary from Mount Vernon

red maple

April

In wet woods and swamps, the **red maple** gives a rosy blush to an otherwise purple and gray treescape. It is a tree which supplies food to many animals: its twigs will be eaten by **white-tailed deer**, its inner bark by **porcupines**, its winged seeds, which come soon after the blossoms fade, by **chipmunks**, **squirrels**, and countless birds.

Blooming at the same time—appearing like a white mist—is the **shadbush**, named for the fish now swimming up streams to spawn. The **redbud** has reddish and purple flowers, is smaller than the maple, and is found in fertile, dry woods and the edges of clearings and roadsides. Its distinctive leaves are heart-shaped. The **wild ginger** flower is difficult to see, since it's hidden at the base of the plant on the forest floor. Look for **trillium** in rich woods; the handsome **purple trillium** has a foul smell that attracts pollinating carrion flies. In the Appalachians a sweeter smelling variety is called "wake-robin."

And of course the **violets**—the pale blue **bird-foot violet** grows under the trees and the **yellow violet** among the leaves.

trillium

CHIPPIES

"Like a flash of brown light," one observer describes the appealing, scampering **chipmunk**. Watch a chipmunk sitting on its haunches and soon it will stop what it's doing and, motionless, watch you.

Spring and fall are the best times to see chipmunks. In winter they're tucked into their burrows with a generous supply of seeds and nuts; on hot summer days they stay below where it's cool. "Chip-chip," calls the chipmunk in alarm. When content, a soft, "kuk-kuk," can be heard for as long as half an hour.

April

In May watch for chipmunk babies to venture up out of the burrows. Sniffing, chasing, pouncing, wrestling, and squealing, spring chippies quickly learn to survive on their own. A second litter will be born in the fall and will spend the winter sleeping underground with the mother; their eyes are closed as they suckle and grow in the burrow. When they emerge, bright-eyed, the stripe on their back will be visible.

FEATHERED FOLK

> *In the beginning, the study of the feathered folk is a delightful torture. There are such a variety of calls and melodies and so many songsters to become familiar with that the novice confounds the call notes and airs of one bird with those of another. If he is content to know just the robin, bluebird, song sparrow, and a few others by sight and song, he gets a mild sort of pleasure from his intercourse with the birds, but if he wishes really to lose himself in this world, he must not only work, but work intelligently. When the bird lover has once mastered the vocabulary of the feathered people he begins to be truly in touch with them.*

CORDELIA STANWOOD

Beyond The Spring by Chandler S. Richmond

Just before dawn, a bird orchestra heralds the sun. All day the **phoebe** flits about for the insects that now have hatched, perches on a branch wagging its tail, and calls out its nasal name, "fee-bee."

rose-breasted grosbeak

April

In the swamp, in secluded recesses,
A shy and hidden bird is warbling a song.
Solitary, the thrush,
The hermit, withdrawn to himself, avoiding the settlements,
Sings by himself a song.

WALT WHITMAN
"When Lilacs Last in the Dooryard Bloom'd"

Listen for the flutelike, melodic cascade of notes the **wood thrush** sings at dawn or dusk. The **veery** whistles a beautiful series of downward spirals. "Cheer up, cheer, cheer, cheer up," chirps a **robin**. Similar but sweeter is the warble of the **rose-breasted grosbeak**, who whistles a long, liquid carol of short, continuous phrases.

A solitary robin hopped to another spot on the lawn, cocked its head, and deftly plucked a worm. Overhead a bluejay scolded, contesting a squirrel's right to the leftover acorns at the foot of the tree. A honey bee reveled in the rich pollen of a daffodil, packing bits of gold into back-leg baskets.

ROGER TORY PETERSON
Gardening With Wildlife

At the river or the brook you can hear the **kingfisher** emits his loud, distinctive, staccato rattle. In the garden a **wren** chatters and scolds. "Sweet, sweet, sweet," sings the **song sparrow**, or "maids, maids, maids, put-on-your-tea-kettle-ettle-ettle," according to Thoreau's description of three short notes and a varied trill. The **white throat**'s song is prettier—one or two clear notes followed by three quavering ones: "sweet, sweet, Canada, Canada, Canada."

April

CHECKLIST—WILDFLOWERS IN THE WOODS

When beechen buds begin to swell,
And woods the blue-bird's warble know,
The yellow violet's modest bell
Peeps from the last year's leaves below.

WILLIAM CULLEN BRYANT
"The Yellow Violet"

☐ bird-foot violet; ☐ bluebell (Virginia cowslip); ☐ bloodroot; ☐ common blue violet; ☐ dogtooth violet (adder's tongue, trout lily); ☐ Dutchman's-breeches; ☐ foam flower; ☐ golden ragwort; ☐ Jack-in-the-pulpit; ☐ Japanese honeysuckle; ☐ larkspur; ☐ marsh marigold; ☐ rue anemone; ☐ spring beauty; ☐ trumpet honeysuckle; ☐ white trillium; ☐ white violet; ☐ wood anemone; ☐ yellow violet.

☐ . . . .   ☐ . . . .   ☐ . . . .
☐ . . . .   ☐ . . . .   ☐ . . . .
☐ . . . .   ☐ . . . .   ☐ . . . .

WILDLIFE CHECKLIST

BIRDS HEARD:

☐ bluebird; ☐ chickadee; ☐ kingfisher; ☐ phoebe; ☐ robin; ☐ rose-breasted grosbeak; ☐ song sparrow; ☐ veery; ☐ warbler; ☐ white-throated sparrow; ☐ wood thrush.

☐ . . . .   ☐ . . . .   ☐ . . . .
☐ . . . .   ☐ . . . .   ☐ . . . .

OTHER ANIMALS:

☐ Chipmunk activity . . . .

. . . .

. . . .

April

☐ bee; ☐ porcupine; ☐ snake; ☐ tadpole; ☐ turtle; ☐ white-tailed deer.

☐ .... ☐ .... ☐ ....

☐ .... ☐ .... ☐ ....

☐ .... ☐ .... ☐ ....

PLANT LIFE:

☐ evergreen; ☐ moss; ☐ partridge berry; ☐ redbud; ☐ red maple;

☐ shadbush; ☐ wild ginger.

white-throated sparrow

April

. . . .
. . . .
. . . .
. . . .
. . . .
. . . .
. . . .
. . . .
. . . .
. . . .
. . . .
. . . .
. . . .
. . . .
. . . .
. . . .
. . . .
. . . .
. . . .
. . . .
. . . .
. . . .
. . . .
. . . .
. . . .
. . . .

May

For lo, the winter is past,
The rain is over and gone;
The flowers appear on the earth;
The time of singing has come,
And the voice of the turtle
Is heard in our land.

Song of Solomon 2:11–12

May

SONGBIRDS

They'll come again to the apple tree—
Robin and all the rest—
When the orchard branches are fair to see
In the snow of the blossoms dressed,
And the prettiest thing in the world will be
The building of the nest.

MARGARET E. SANGSTER

"The Building of the Nest"

In spring songbirds return from the South driven by the greatest of urges, as the increasing light of the season stimulates their hormones and reproductive systems, compelling the birds to hurry north to breed. Most songbirds pair for the raising of one brood or for the entire breeding season.

COURTING. Although the food supply on the way north decides the pace of migration, the males always arrive first to establish their territories. When the females appear, they wander in and out of these territories for several days as the males compete for their attention:

scarlet tanager

the **evening grosbeak** dances; the **cardinal** raises his crest; the **oriole** and shy **scarlet tanager** parade; and the **kinglet** and **kingbird** display bright crown patches. The male **cedar waxwing**, **goldfinch**, and **bluebird** court with food offerings, while the **yellow-billed cuckoo** actually feeds his mate while copulating.

May

NESTING. Once she's accepted her mate, the female usually chooses a nesting site (it's been observed that no female **redstart warbler** ever chose a site that she had been "directed" to by a male). Songbirds create cup-shaped nests, above ground, and build new ones for each set of eggs.

*Waxwings and **bank swallow** males share equally in the task of construction. The female **robin** does the building from materials supplied by her partner. A **red-eyed vireo** and **oven-bird** female work alone, while the male **wren** builds a few dummy nests before his mate finally chooses one to complete.*

*Wonderfully crafted nests are formed by the vireo, **flycatcher**, and **goldfinch**, and the nest of the **oriole** is a pendulous creation. Foundations are of twigs interwoven with grasses, weeds, strips of bark, leaves, and pine needles. The **robin** and **wood thrush** hold their nests together with mud. A soft lining is made from moss, animal hairs, feathers, and plant down.*

HATCHING. Just after sunrise the songbirds lay their fertilized eggs, one each day until the clutch is complete. The incubating birds (the duller colored females, usually) have a featherless patch on their belly through which body heat is transferred, and they turn their eggs to maintain an even temperature. The male brings food to the nest-bound mate. If the eggs are destroyed by an invader, they will start again.

Two or three days before hatching the fetus pierces an air chamber within the egg and begins breathing. A powerful muscle on its head helps it "pip" the shell with the "egg tooth" on the tip of its bill. Several hours, or even days, of pipping and resting go on until the peeping baby bird emerges. The parents are ready and waiting with food and tidy up the nest by removing the cracked shells.

May

When I examine the fragile, gem-like eggs from which these rare creatures [chestnut-sided warbler] emerge and observe the fledglings flitting through the trees in a little over a week from the time they pip the shells, I feel as if the day of miracles is still at hand. It makes every thicket, every hedge, every woodland a wonderful spot since I do not know how many such miracles every briar patch may conceal.

CORDELIA STANWOOD

Beyond The Spring by Chandler S. Richmond

house
wren

NESTLINGS. Songbirds remain nestlings for a week or two. The parents, at first, "brood" their helpless, naked young to protect them from the elements, feeding them continuously from early morning to evening. (A **house wren** was seen bringing food home every six minutes.) Cardinals prefer grains and fruits for themselves, but stuff protein-rich insects down the throats of their young. Birds must take great care of their feathers, and so nestlings learn to preen before they leave the nest.

FLIGHT. On the first flight, a parent may fly just below or just above the adventuresome youngster. Few fledgling songbirds will return to the nest when flight is mastered (except wrens and swallows), but they may need food from the elders for a few days more.

In time the young bird perfects its flight skills—tail as rudder, wind for alighting and taking off—and gradually drifts away from its parents to live and forage on its own.

May

FROGS AND TOADS

By now the toads and frogs are in full voice. A frog is smooth skinned, a toad has warts. The frog lays eggs in a cloudy mass, the toad in a long string. When you walk along a stream, green frogs hide in the mud or jump in the water, swimming rapidly away with their long, agile legs. Toads are more terrestrial and prefer cool, moist places, but can be found in deserts as well as in forests, mountains, fields, and gardens.

Both hibernate all winter and lay their eggs in water in the spring. Tadpoles hatch from the eggs and begin their amazing metamorphosis from under water gill-breathers with tails to tail-less air-breathers with legs.

Although it lives on low bushes or rushes in swamps and ponds, the **spring peeper**, with an X mark on its tiny back, is classified as a tree frog. **Cricket** and **chorus frogs** are southern cousins. They call to their mates with their musical piping made by pumping air into a vocal sac in the throat. A **bull frog** is six times larger.

The **salamander**, a night-hunting amphibian with a tail, can be found in damp leaves and under rotting logs. Her eggs are laid singly in jelly. After a rain you may see a red-spotted **newt**, unusual because of its three stages of metamorphosis, not two: larva (in water with gills); salamander or eft (on land with lungs and orange-red spots); and after three years, newt (in water but surfaces for air).

frog

CHECKLIST

☐ bull frog; ☐ cardinal; ☐ chorus frog; ☐ cricket frog; ☐ evening grosbeak; ☐ fly catcher; ☐ goldfinch; ☐ house wren; ☐ kingbird; ☐ kinglet; ☐ newt; ☐ oriole; ☐ oven-bird; ☐ redstart warbler; ☐ salamander; ☐ scarlet tanager; ☐ spring peeper; ☐ vireo; ☐ waxwing.

May

> *And buttercups are coming,*
> *and scarlet columbine,*
> *And in the sunny meadows*
> *The dandelions shine.*
>
> CELIA THAXTER
>
> *"Spring"*

Poets rhapsodize over May, and no wonder— with the forest floor suddenly carpeted with such treasures as these:

☐ azalea; ☐ blueberry; ☐ bluet (Quaker ladies); ☐ bunchberry; ☐ butter and eggs; ☐ buttercup; ☐ Canada mayflower (wild lily of the valley); ☐ cherry; ☐ climbing nightshade; ☐ columbine; ☐ corydalis; ☐ crab-apples; ☐ dandelion; ☐ dogwood; ☐ fleabane; ☐ hawthorne trees; ☐ hedge bindweed; ☐ highbush; ☐ hobblebush; ☐ lady's-slipper; ☐ laurel; ☐ May apple; ☐ white mayster (starflower); ☐ phlox; ☐ plum; ☐ prickly poppy; ☐ red clover; ☐ rhododendron; ☐ smooth and false Solomon's seal; ☐ wild strawberry; ☐ viburnum; ☐ wisteria vines.

☐ . . . . ☐ . . . .
☐ . . . . ☐ . . . .
☐ . . . . ☐ . . . .
☐ . . . . ☐ . . . .
☐ . . . . ☐ . . . .
☐ . . . . ☐ . . . .
☐ . . . . ☐ . . . .
☐ . . . . ☐ . . . .
☐ . . . . ☐ . . . .
☐ . . . . ☐ . . . .

lady's-slipper

May

columbine

May

June

And what is so rare as a day in June?
Then, if ever, come perfect days.

JAMES RUSSELL LOWELL
"The Vision of Sir Launfal"

June

EMBLEM OF SUMMER: THE BUTTERFLY

Embodying freedom, beauty, and transience,
the butterfly seems the perfect image of
summer. Our universal wonder about them
persists despite—or is it because of—the short
time they are with us. The life spans of butterflies are not thoroughly understood, but we know
they are short and vary among species. The flight

monarch butterfly

period of most broods is from thirty to forty days, and
no individual butterfly lives the full span of that time. There are, however,
butterflies that live only three to four days and certain **monarch** butterflies
that may live up to six months.

A common misconception is that butterflies and **moths** are easily distin-
guished from each other. In fact they are very similar, and the differences
subtle. Butterflies fly by day and have antennae with a club (swelling) at the
tip. Moths are largely nocturnal, stouter in body than daytime butterflies, and
have feathered antennae that taper to a fine point. Perhaps least understood
is that many butterflies have dull, dingy coloring that we associate with moths,
while many moths wear colors as brilliant as any butterfly.

Colors on butterflies function as either protection or declaration. Some
colors are used to camouflage them from prey against a backdrop of tree bark
or leaves, such as the dull colors on **skippers**. Other butterflies with dramatic,
contrasting coloring are meant to loudly proclaim who they are—especially
to predators. Monarchs, like many butterflies, are unpalatable to their
predators due to poisons within their bodies. Birds, lizards, and dragonflies
prey on butterflies while the main predators of butterfly larvae are parasites.

Butterfly courtship displays involve intricate aerial maneuvers. A few make
sounds—loud clicking noises heard one hundred feet away—that humans can
hear.

June

Butterflies are often seen basking in the sun. Basking, with wings spread, is necessary to raise their body temperatures above 80 degrees Fahrenheit, to tune their wing muscles, and to give them energy for flight. The warmed blood circulating in their wing veins travels to the rest of their bodies. On very hot days they keep cool by closing their wings and aligning them so only the top edges are exposed to the sun; they also breathe rapidly, drink from water drops, and find shade like the rest of us.

The best documented butterfly migrations are of **painted ladies** and monarchs. Painted ladies move up from Mexico to the United States and into Canada by summer. Monarchs fly in established routes down the length of North America. How they orient themselves over thousands of miles of widely varied terrain remains unclear.

WILDLIFE IN THE MOONLIT SUMMER

The handsome **skunk**'s notorious, noxious spray is stored in two glands under its tail. Before discharging it at an enemy, the skunk stamps its feet and growls. In midsummer youngsters follow their mother single file as she meanders about the feeding ground.

The North American pink-nosed marsupial, the **opossum**, was roaming the continent sixty million years ago. After birth, opossum babies crawl with their forepaws into the mother's abdominal pouch and ride there. Those who find a nipple and hang onto it for some seventy days survive and mature. Later, they hitch rides on their mother's back.

Known for "playing opossum," they go into a momentary state of shock when threatened. Pulse and heartbeat slow, eyes close, and tongue hangs out. An opossum is the only wild animal in the United States that can hang by its tail, a tail that also comes in handy for carrying leaves to the nest. Big, thumblike toes and fifty teeth (the most of any North American land animal) help the opossum gather food. A footprint reveals that one of its toes is angled.

June

The **raccoon** hunts at night and is partial to fruits and vegetables and small, water animals. (It is mostly captive raccoons that wash their food before eating it, says Madeline Angell in *America's Best Loved Wild Animals*.) During July, babies will follow their mother on nightly forages. By day, raccoons and opossums usually rest in hollow trees. The skunk doesn't climb trees, so mother and babies sleep in an underground den.

At dusk listen for the **whippoorwill**, who can call its name once a second; at night, by a lake or bay, hear the yodel of the **loon**. Active in the marshes are the **woodcock**, **bittern**, and **night heron**. In the woods are the **great horned owl**, the **screech owl**, and the **barred owl**. Nocturnal **bats** are the only flying mammal (**flying squirrels** actually glide from tree to tree). Adult humans can't hear the bat's high-frequency "sonar" sound, but children often can. Highly visible, night-flying insects include the **June bug** (a beetle), **firefly** (also a beetle), and the soft-green **luna moth**.

raccoon

*The fireflies
o'er the meadow
In pulses come and go.*
JAMES RUSSELL LOWELL
"Midnight"

CHECKLIST—THE MEADOWS

*It's surely summer, for there's a swallow;
Come one swallow, his mate will follow,
The bird race quicken and wheel and thicken.*

CHRISTINA G. ROSSETTI

"A Bird Song"

June

BIRDS:

☐ bobolink; ☐ bobwhite; ☐ chipping sparrow; ☐ cuckoo;

☐ field sparrow; ☐ quail; ☐ meadowlark; ☐ swallow; ☐ swift.

☐ . . . . ☐ . . . . ☐ . . . .

☐ . . . . ☐ . . . . ☐ . . . .

BUTTERFLIES:

☐ blue; ☐ fritillary; ☐ hairstreak; ☐ monarch; ☐ painted lady;

☐ skipper; ☐ swallowtail.

☐ . . . . ☐ . . . . ☐ . . . .

☐ . . . . ☐ . . . . ☐ . . . .

GRASSES:

☐ bluegrass; ☐ Kentucky; ☐ redtop; ☐ timothy.

☐ . . . . ☐ . . . . ☐ . . . .

PLANT LIFE:

☐ bee balm; ☐ blue-eyed grass; ☐ butterfly weed;

☐ Canada lily; ☐ chicory; ☐ common mullein;

☐ daisy; ☐ dayflower; ☐ deptford pink; ☐ harebell;

☐ mustard; ☐ milkweed; ☐ lupine; ☐ maiden
(or meadow) pink; ☐ Queen Anne's lace;

☐ ragged robin (New England); ☐ St. John's
wort; ☐ tall meadow rue; ☐ thistle; ☐ wild rose.

☐ . . . . ☐ . . . .

☐ . . . . ☐ . . . .

☐ . . . . ☐ . . . .

☐ . . . . ☐ . . . .

☐ . . . . ☐ . . . .

blue-eyed grass

June

CHECKLIST—NEAR THE WATER

She rears her young on yonder tree,
She leaves her faithful mate to mind 'em,
Like us, for fish, she sails to sea,
And, plunging, shows us where to find 'em

ALEXANDER WILSON

"Kingfisher" from *"The Fisherman's Hymn"*

BIRDS:

☐ common snipe; ☐ egret; ☐ fish crow; ☐ great blue heron; ☐ grebe;

☐ green heron; ☐ kingfisher; ☐ marsh wren; ☐ rail; ☐ swamp sparrow.

☐ . . . .   ☐ . . . .   ☐ . . . .

☐ . . . .   ☐ . . . .   ☐ . . . .

☐ . . . .   ☐ . . . .   ☐ . . . .

WILDFLOWERS:

☐ blue flag; ☐ buttonbush; ☐ cattail;

☐ forget-me-nots; ☐ horsetail;

☐ pickerel weed; ☐ swamp loosestrife;

☐ wild leek; ☐ yellow flag.

☐ . . . .

☐ . . . .

☐ . . . .

☐ . . . .

☐ . . . .

☐ . . . .

☐ . . . .

☐ . . . .

☐ . . . .

green heron

June

> As I looked about me I felt that the grass was
> the country, as the water is the sea. The red
> of the grass made all the great prairie the color
> of wine-stains, or of certain seaweeds when
> they are first washed up. And there was so much
> motion in it; the whole country seemed, somehow,
> to be running.
>
> WILLA CATHER
>
> *My Antonia*

prairie coneflower

ANIMALS:

□ badger; □ bison; □ bullsnake; □ burrowing owl; □ coyote;
□ ferruginous hawk; □ ferret; □ grasshopper sparrow; □ ground
squirrel; □ horned lark; □ horney toad; □ jack rabbit; □ meadowlark;
□ mourning dove; □ prairie chicken; □ prairie dog; □ prairie falcon;
□ prairie rattlesnake; □ pronghorn (antelope); □ quail; □ red-tailed
hawk; □ sandhill crane; □ scissor-tailed flycatcher.

□ . . . .   □ . . . .   □ . . . .
□ . . . .   □ . . . .   □ . . . .
□ . . . .   □ . . . .   □ . . . .
□ . . . .   □ . . . .   □ . . . .

GRASSES AND WILDFLOWERS:

□ big bluegrass; □ black-eyed Susan; □ buffalo grass; □ cat claw;
□ compass plant; □ goldenrod; □ gumweed broom; □ Illinois tick
trefoil; □ Indian blanket; □ locoweed; □ mesquite; □ pasqueflowers;
□ porcupine grass; □ prairie clover; □ prairie coneflower; □ prairie
golden aster; □ prairie June grass; □ prairie larkspur; □ prairie mimosa;

June

☐ prairie rose; ☐ prairie smoke; ☐ prairie wild indigo; ☐ prickly poppy; ☐ snake weed; ☐ sunflower; ☐ switch grass; ☐ Texas bluebonnet; ☐ windmill grass.

☐ . . . . ☐ . . . . ☐ . . . .

☐ . . . . ☐ . . . . ☐ . . . .

☐ . . . . ☐ . . . . ☐ . . . .

☐ . . . . ☐ . . . . ☐ . . . .

☐ . . . . ☐ . . . . ☐ . . . .

. . . .

. . . .

. . . .

. . . .

. . . .

. . . .

. . . .

. . . .

. . . .

. . . .

. . . .

. . . .

. . . .

. . . .

. . . .

. . . .

. . . .

July

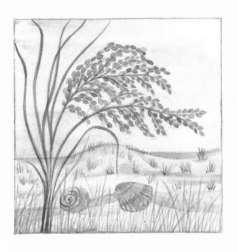

The tide rises, the tide falls,
The twilight darkens, the curlew calls;
Along the sea-sands damp and brown
The traveller hastens toward the town,
And the tide rises, the tide falls.

HENRY WADSWORTH LONGFELLOW
"The Tide Rises, The Tide Falls"

July

SEASIDE AND SHORE

Spring tides—having the greatest range of rise
and fall—come twice a month, at the full moon
and the new moon when sun, moon, and earth are
nearly aligned. Neap tides—with the lowest range—
occur at the end of the first and third quarter
when moon and sun are at right angles to each
other.

sea lavendar

> *The first ripples of incoming tide bring the petrified [barnacle]*
> *fields to life. Then, if one stands ankle-deep in water and observes*
> *closely, one sees tiny shadows flickering everywhere over the*
> *submerged rocks.*
>
> RACHEL CARSON
> *The Edge of the Sea*

Clams are found in mudflats, but look for their shells along the shore.
Quahog is an American Indian name for the hard (or round) clam. Young
ones are **little neck clams** or **cherrystones**. Look too for the **soft** (long)
clam, the **razor**, and the **surf** (sea) clam. On the edge of the water from New
Jersey south is the **coquina**. Flat **sand dollars**, members of the sea urchin
family, burrow in the sand.

> *There was a salt-marsh that bounded part of the*
> *millpond, on the edge of which, at high water, we*
> *used to stand to fish for minnows…*
>
> BENJAMIN FRANKLIN
> *Autobiography*

July

On rocky coasts distinctive life can be seen descending from high and dry rock to low-tide shore, ranging from colonies of blue-green **algae**, which actually look black, to **Irish moss**, **barnacles**, and **limpets**.

A limpet is a snail which browses in its small territory, then returns to its home, a rounded depression in a rock. On a low-tide beach you can see snail trails in the mud.

Rockweed holds fast to rocks near shore; "balloons" on its leathery fronds keep it floating on the tide. A **blue mussel** crawls to rockweed "jungles" with a long, tubular foot, then spins golden threads which anchor it in several directions. A **periwinkle** snail clings to rocks, too, and with toothed tongue scrapes off layers of plant cells. On rockweed fronds it lays its eggs in a stiff jelly. Baby periwinkles are hatched fully formed.

WATERSIDE SENTINELS—EAGLE AND OSPREY

At the top of a spruce tree on a cliff overlooking a bay, pond, or river, the **bald eagle** often takes its perch. In similar environs the **osprey** (fish hawk) is seen and often mistaken for the eagle. A pure white head marks the mature eagle. The osprey's head has some white, but a black mask crosses its face.

Watch them soar. The eagle's belly is dark, its tail white. The osprey's tail is dark, its belly white. Wingspans on both are awesome: nearly seven feet for the flat-winged bald eagle, four to six feet for the osprey, whose wings have a slight kink. Close up, the eagle's beak, toes, and eyes are bright yellow. Its call is like the gull's—a squeaky cackle. The osprey makes a persistent, cheeping whistle.

osprey

July

Both are fish eaters. Plunging feet-first, the osprey's four hooked talons grip and securely lock into its prey. The bird carries the fish's head forward to minimize wind resistance. If an eagle spots the osprey it may rob it of a meal in midair. Both the eagle and osprey carry their catch up to a perch, anchor it with talons, and skillfully carve it with hooked beaks nearly as large as their heads.

Ospreys are one of the most widely distributed birds, found on almost every continent. The northerners migrate south, while bald eagles usually winter over. Both build or repair enormous, bulky stick nests with their mates. Look far up in a tall tree for an eagle nest; it may be as high as 150 feet. A charming sight is an osprey nest perched on a channel marker with three babies exercising their wings.

CHECKLIST—IN THE WATER

We fish, we fish, we merrily swim
We care not for friend nor for foe.
Our fins are stout,
Our tails are out,
As through the seas we go.

HERMAN MELVILLE
"We Fish"

☐ crab; ☐ finback whale; ☐ dolphins; ☐ gray seal; ☐ harbor seal; ☐ lobster; ☐ oyster; ☐ scallop; ☐ sea cucumber; ☐ sea turtle; ☐ starfish.

☐ . . . . ☐ . . . . ☐ . . . .

☐ . . . . ☐ . . . . ☐ . . . .

☐ . . . . ☐ . . . . ☐ . . . .

☐ . . . . ☐ . . . . ☐ . . . .

☐ . . . . ☐ . . . . ☐ . . . .

July

> *At high tide the gulls rest on ledges of rock, dry above the surf and*
> *the spray, and they tuck their yellow bills under their feathers and*
> *doze away the hours of the rising water.*
>
> RACHEL CARSON
> *The Edge of the Sea*

☐ bald eagle; ☐ brown pelican (south and west coasts); ☐ common
egret; ☐ cormorant (Northeast); ☐ fish crow; gulls (☐ Bonaparte,
☐ great, ☐ black-backed, ☐ herring, ☐ laughing); herons (☐ black-
crowned night, ☐ green, ☐ little blue, ☐ Louisiana); ☐ loon;
☐ osprey; ☐ sandpiper; ☐ tern.

☐ . . . .   ☐ . . . .   ☐ . . . .
☐ . . . .   ☐ . . . .   ☐ . . . .

SHORE PLANTS:

☐ bayberry; ☐ beach heather; ☐ beach pea; ☐ beach plum; ☐ bearberry;
☐ glassworts; ☐ prickly pear; ☐ rugosa rose; ☐ sea lavender; ☐ sea oats;
☐ sea rocket; ☐ seaside goldenrod.

☐ . . . .   ☐ . . . .
☐ . . . .   ☐ . . . .

. . . .
. . . .
. . . .
. . . .
. . . .
. . . .
. . . .
. . . .

herring gull

July

TIDAL POOL LIFE:

> *Tide pools contain mysterious worlds within their depths, where all the beauty of the sea is subtly suggested and portrayed in miniature.*

> RACHEL CARSON
>
> *The Edge of the Sea*

☐ blue mussel ☐ crab; ☐ sea anemone; ☐ sea urchin; ☐ starfish.

☐ . . . . ☐ . . . . ☐ . . . .

☐ . . . . ☐ . . . . ☐ . . . .

. . . .

. . . .

AT THE STRAND LINE (JUST ABOVE HIGH TIDE):

☐ blackened rockweed; ☐ crab shell; ☐ sand hopper (beach fly);

☐ seastraw; ☐ skates' egg case (mermaid purse).

☐ . . . . ☐ . . . . ☐ . . . .

☐ . . . . ☐ . . . . ☐ . . . .

. . . .

. . . .

IN THE EELGRASS AT WATER'S EDGE:

☐ bay scallop; ☐ crab; ☐ eel; ☐ horseshoe crab; ☐ limpet; ☐ mussel;

☐ periwinkle; ☐ pipe fish; ☐ sea horse; ☐ slipper shell.

☐ . . . . ☐ . . . . ☐ . . . .

☐ . . . . ☐ . . . . ☐ . . . .

. . . .

. . . .

. . . .

July

THE ALPINE AND TUNDRA REGIONS

In the high mountains of national parks of the West are animals seen nowhere else—such outsized members of the deer family as the **wapiti** (American elk), the **Alaska moose**, and the **caribou**.

A male wapiti can weigh up to 1,000 pounds, has five-foot, branched antlers, a distinctive tan and yellow patch on his rump, and a brown mane on his neck. The Alaska moose is the world's largest deer, weighing almost a ton, and bearing broad, flat, eighty-five pound antlers. A flap of skin hangs from a moose's throat like a bell. **Caribou** in Mount McKinley National Park, Alaska, are smaller, white-maned relatives of reindeer (introduced from Europe) and are the only deer whose females have antlers.

Wintering herds of deer families migrate to higher ground and separate in spring into small groups of bulls and bands of pregnant or single cows. Nursing fawns stay with their mothers throughout the summer, gradually learning to forage at night for food. Elk feed in alpine meadows, moose in lakes and swamps, and caribou on lichen and moss of the treeless tundra.

At one time sixty million hump-shouldered **bison** (American buffalo) grazed on the plains of North America; by 1900, only 300 were left in the United States. Herds are making a comeback at Yellowstone National Park and the Wichita Mountains Wildlife Preserve. Bison have short, curved horns, shaggy brown hair on front legs and shoulders, massive heads, and beards. A male may weigh a ton. Huge as they are, bison can run up to 35 miles per hour, make quick turns, and climb up and run down steep mountains. Another kind of wild cattle, the **musk oxen**, live in arctic North America.

Bearded **mountain goats** wearing white, shaggy coats are slow, methodical climbers. They have two toes that act as pliers and pads between them that act as suction cups. Goats carefully pull themselves up rock faces above the tree line to nibble on alpine plants, lichen, mosses, and scrub.

July

Bighorn sheep bound swiftly up almost vertical cliffs, zigzagging from one two-inch foothold to another. Coming down, they half leap, half fall as much as twenty feet. An elastic hoof-covering grips surfaces and helps absorb the shock. A creamy white rump patch is conspicuous in the brown hair (not wool) of both females and males. The ram's powerful horns curve back and around almost to a full circle. (White-coated **dall sheep** have flared horns and live in arctic Alaska and Canada, as do **polar bears**.

A type of brown bear, **grizzly bears** are found at Yellowstone or Glacier National Parks. The **Alaska brown bear** fishes for spawning salmon at Mount McKinley Park in July. Standing upright, this giant fisherman towers to nine feet, the world's largest carnivore.

CHECKLIST—THE ALPINE AND TUNDRA REGIONS

ANIMALS:

☐ American elk; ☐ arctic hare; ☐ arctic fox; ☐ bighorn sheep; ☐ bison; ☐ caribou; ☐ dall sheep; ☐ Douglas squirrel; ☐ falcon; ☐ golden eagle; ☐ gray jay; ☐ lemming; ☐ moose; ☐ mountain goat; ☐ musk oxen; ☐ pika (cony); ☐ pipit; ☐ ptarmigan; ☐ yellow-belly marmot.

☐ . . . .   ☐ . . . .   ☐ . . . .

☐ . . . .   ☐ . . . .   ☐ . . . .

☐ . . . .   ☐ . . . .   ☐ . . . .

TREES:

☐ aspen; ☐ blue spruce; ☐ Douglas fir; ☐ lodgepole pine; ☐ limber pine; ☐ mountain hemlock; ☐ ponderosa pine; ☐ Sitka spruce; ☐ subalpine fir; ☐ western red cedar.

☐ . . . .   ☐ . . . .   ☐ . . . .

☐ . . . .   ☐ . . . .   ☐ . . . .

☐ . . . .   ☐ . . . .   ☐ . . . .

July

WILDFLOWERS:

☐ alpine azalea; ☐ alpine bearberry; ☐ alpine forget-me-nots; ☐ avalanche lily; ☐ balsamroot; ☐ bear (or squaw) grass; ☐ blue columbine; ☐ blue lupine; ☐ fawn lily; ☐ fleabane; ☐ Indian paint brush; ☐ larkspur; ☐ monkey flower; ☐ moss campion; ☐ mountain buttercup; ☐ mountain daisy; ☐ penstemon; ☐ pink heather; ☐ potentilla; ☐ ruff and blue-green gentian; ☐ scarlet gilia; ☐ shooting star; ☐ wild buckwheat; ☐ wild geranium.

☐ . . . .   ☐ . . . .   ☐ . . . .
☐ . . . .   ☐ . . . .   ☐ . . . .
☐ . . . .   ☐ . . . .   ☐ . . . .
☐ . . . .   ☐ . . . .   ☐ . . . .
☐ . . . .   ☐ . . . .   ☐ . . . .

mountain goat

July

August

The beauteous dragonfly's dancing
By the waves of the rivulet glancing;
She dances here and she dances there,
The glimmering, glittering flutterer fair.

HEINRICH HEINE
"The Dragonfly"

August

THE GLADES

On muggy, midsummer days it seems as if there's nothing in the woods but mosquitoes. But look again. Under a lichen-covered rock a **salamander** or red newt is hiding; from a pile of damp leaves hops a **toad**, while the **timber rattler** prefers dry lands and the **copperhead** suns on wooded hillsides and rocks. Slithering rapidly by, the **black racer** is one of the fastest snakes you will see. The charming **woodland jumping mouse** can leap six feet.

Watch also for the **box turtle**, which can close itself up on its hinged and domed shell. Catch a glimpse of its eyes—the males' are usually red, the females' brown. Notice also the tiny, flying insects that light on the flowers. Some are wildly patterned and colored—miniature dragons in shady woods and sunny clearings. **Insect larvae** may look fierce under a magnifying lens; the larva of the **golden-eye lacewing** is aptly called an aphid lion.

Looking closer, you will see the mosses and the mushrooms, the **Indian pipe**, **hoary mountain mint**, and **horse balm**, the **woodland sunflower**, **pipsissewa**, and **wild senna**. **False Solomon's seal** berries appear gold at a distance, but are pale green speckled with red. The **smooth Solomon's seal** is blue-black and hangs from an arching stem. Along the forest litter are **ground pine** (club moss), **running cedar**, **acorns**, **earthworms**, **snails**, **slugs**, **woodlice**, and **millipedes**. Nestling in rock crevices and between tree roots are graceful ferns: the **ostrich**, **cinnamon**, **maidenhair**, and **royal sensitive**.

As cold weather approaches thousands of black spore cases will dot the undersides of fern fronds. With the first frost, the sensitive fern's leaves disappear; the spore holders on

false Solomon's seal

August

the remaining stalk are brown. Mushrooms spring up overnight after a rain, some with gills (radiating membranes) under their caps; the rest have pores. Look for **parasol**, **boletus**, **gypsy**, **Caeser's**, and **destroying angel**.

SHALLOW BROOK AND PLACID POND

Along quiet streams and ponds grow **cardinal flower**, **swamp smartweed**, **cattails**, **arrowhead** (arrowleaf), **turtlehead**, and in warm climates, **water hyacinth**. Look for **soft rush** in marshy places and **jointed horsetails** (scouring rush), whose giant ancestors, like club mosses, lived 300 million years ago and decomposed to become coal.

The **dragonfly** and **damselfly** are almost doubles, but the dragonfly spreads its wings when at rest, while the damsel's wings are folded over a long, "darning needle" body. (The **caddis fly**, a mothlike insect found near the water, also holds its wings above its body like a roof.) Adults of both often fly in tandem; by the end of August the larger ones have begun to migrate south.

> *A river gorge can be enjoyed*
> *In very many ways.*
> *For instance, many little friends*
> *Are with us nights and days.*
>
> *I favor the mosquitoes*
> *Because they are the food*
> *That nurtures lovely dragonflies,*
> *Well engineered and good.*
>
> *Two others come from larvae,*
> *Crawl on a rock and split.*
> *The mayfly lasts a day or so;*
> *For him or her, that's it.*

August

And stoneflies strip their cover,
Quite oversized of wing.
They flop and fly quite easily,
A most uncanny thing.

The crafty fisher spider
At water's edge will wait
And pluck a minnow from the drink
Without a line or bait.

I love insects and spiders
I praise them highly, too,
For they can do so many things
That I could never do.

MORTON P. MATTHEW

IN FIELDS AND MEADOWS

There is a subtle difference between a field and a meadow. The first is open, cleared land suitable for pasture or cultivation. The second is natural grassland which can be used for pasture. The difference, however, is slight enough to warrant using them interchangeably.

In the meadows beetles are flourishing: the aquatic **whirligig** and **diving beetles**, **ladybugs**, **fireflies**, **wood-boring beetles**, **tumble bugs** (scarab), **Japanese beetles**, and the plant-feeding **potato beetles** and **boll weevils**. **Carrion beetles** are especially fascinating. Some can dig beneath a dead mouse or other small animal until it's buried, then lay their eggs on top of the carcass.

Another field dweller, the American **garter snake**, with brightly colored, lengthwise stripes, got its name years ago from the patterned garters fashionable at the time.

August

The Feathered "Helicopter"

Fluttering and hovering over fields and meadows, darting in and around brightly colored flowers, the **hummingbird** is the smallest North American

hummingbird

bird. In the sun the **ruby-throat**'s body is metallic green and the male's iridescent throat is red—a brilliant sight. The wide-ranging hummingbird, partial to red, seeks out columbine in the spring, bee balm, jewelweed, and trumpet creeper in the summer, and trumpet honeysuckle from May to frost. Many flowers depend on the hummingbird for pollination. A slender, pointed bill can reach deep within a flower for nectar (carbohydrate to the hummingbird); insects and spiders provide protein.

This tiny bird is world famous for its remarkable agility and speed. Timed in flight at fifty to sixty miles per hour, it also can fly backward, up and down, and sideways, and suddenly stop and then start again. While hovering to feed, the ruby-throat's wings beat fifty-five times a second! To defend its territory and in courtship, the male makes "spectacular, swinging, pendulum-like aerial flights," writes John Terres in the *Audubon Encyclopedia*. Watch this fiercely defensive midget drive away others of its kind, as well as **bumblebees**, **hawk moths**, **kingbirds**, **crows**, and even **eagles**. The female is just as aggressive at defending her compact, walnut-sized nest and two-egg broods.

Because of its high metabolism, the hummingbird has to feed all day (a small crop holds nourishment for the night). At the end of summer the ruby-throat in your garden is fueling up for the trip south 600 miles across the Gulf of Mexico to Costa Rica.

August

FLY FACTS

The females of the **black fly, mosquito,** and **horsefly** species eat blood because they need extra nourishment for their eggs. **Housefly** larvae eat decaying material; **robber flies** eat other insects. **Fruit flies** destroy orchard fruits, and **flower flies** look and buzz like bees and wasps but don't sting.

ANT COLONIES

The busy ants of summer live in colonies under the ground or in natural cavities, in numbers from a few dozen to hundreds of thousands. After the mating flight with the queen, the males die. The queen then sheds her wings and lays eggs over a period that may last fifteen years. Workers (wingless females) provide food—consisting of liquids from plants and animals such as the honeydew or the excretion of aphids (sap-sucking insects). These aphids are moved by the worker ants from plant to plant and brought to the nest in winter.

SPIDERS

Fangs, four pairs of walking legs, and eight eyes equip spiders for survival. A **hunting spider** stays out at night; a **harvestman** (daddy longlegs) can be seen on the daytime prowl. The **wolf spider** is stealthy, and the **house spider** ensnares its prey with a flat, sheetlike web; the **garden spider**'s orbed web catches flying insects. A **trapwire spider** hides in a tube in its radial web and quickly emerges when it feels a victim's vibrations on the silken threads. The silk also comes in handy for protective egg cases and for climbing up and down in the air.

GRASSHOPPER AND FAMILY

The **walking stick**, a grasshopper relative that doesn't jump, is a plant eater masquerading as a twig. The finger-length, thicker-bodied **praying mantis**

August

waits for its victims as if in prayer. The **grasshopper** and **katydid** are hard to tell apart; the katydid is greener, has long hind legs and antennae. A grasshopper has a larger head, longer abdomen, and a double pair of wings.

CHECKLIST

WILDLIFE IN FOREST GLADES:

☐ black racer snake; ☐ box turtle; ☐ copperhead; ☐ earthworms; ☐ golden-eye lacewing larva; ☐ insect larvae; ☐ millipedes; ☐ woodland jumping mouse; ☐ woodlice.

☐ . . . .   ☐ . . . .   ☐ . . . .
☐ . . . .   ☐ . . . .   ☐ . . . .
☐ . . . .   ☐ . . . .   ☐ . . . .
☐ . . . .   ☐ . . . .   ☐ . . . .
☐ . . . .   ☐ . . . .   ☐ . . . .

PLANT LIFE IN FOREST GLADES:

☐ acorns; ☐ bay-scented (boulder); ☐ boletus mushroom; ☐ Caeser's mushroom; ☐ cinnamon fern; ☐ destroying angel mushroom; ☐ false Solomon's seal; ☐ ground pine (club moss); ☐ hemlock; ☐ hoary mountain mint; ☐ horse balm; ☐ Indian pipe; ☐ interrupted fern; ☐ maple; ☐ maidenhair fern; ☐ oak; ☐ ostrich fern; ☐ parasol mushroom; ☐ pipsissewa; ☐ royal sensitive fern; ☐ white wood aster; ☐ wild senna; ☐ woodland sunflower.

☐ . . . .   ☐ . . . .   ☐ . . . .
☐ . . . .   ☐ . . . .   ☐ . . . .
☐ . . . .   ☐ . . . .   ☐ . . . .
☐ . . . .   ☐ . . . .   ☐ . . . .
☐ . . . .   ☐ . . . .   ☐ . . . .
☐ . . . .   ☐ . . . .   ☐ . . . .

August

WILDLIFE IN OR NEAR WATER:

☐ aquatic beetles; ☐ bass; ☐ backswimmer bug; ☐ caddis fly; ☐ carp; ☐ catfish; ☐ crayfish; ☐ damselfly; ☐ dragonfly; ☐ floating snails; ☐ fresh water mussels; ☐ frog; ☐ minnow; ☐ painted turtle; ☐ perch; ☐ pickerel; ☐ pike; ☐ red-eared turtle; ☐ snapping turtle; ☐ spotted turtle; ☐ sturgeon; ☐ water boatman bug; ☐ trout; ☐ water scorpion; ☐ water snake; ☐ water strider beetle.

☐ . . . . ☐ . . . . ☐ . . . .

☐ . . . . ☐ . . . . ☐ . . . .

☐ . . . . ☐ . . . . ☐ . . . .

☐ . . . . ☐ . . . . ☐ . . . .

PLANT LIFE IN OR NEAR WATER:

☐ arrowhead; ☐ cardinal flower; ☐ jointed horsetails; ☐ soft rush; ☐ swamp smartweed; ☐ turtleweed; ☐ water hyacinth.

☐ . . . . ☐ . . . .

☐ . . . . ☐ . . . .

☐ . . . . ☐ . . . .

cardinal flower

WILDLIFE IN FIELDS AND MEADOWS:

☐ ant; ☐ black fly; ☐ boll weevil; ☐ bumblebee; ☐ crows; ☐ diving beetle; ☐ eagle; ☐ flower fly; ☐ fruit fly; ☐ garden spider; ☐ garter snake; ☐ grasshopper; ☐ harvestman spider (daddy longlegs); ☐ hawk moth; ☐ horsefly; ☐ housefly; ☐ house spider; ☐ hummingbird; ☐ hunting spider; ☐ Japanese beetle; ☐ katydid; ☐ kingbird; ☐ ladybug; ☐ mosquito; ☐ potato beetle; ☐ praying mantis; ☐ robber fly; ☐ ruby-throated hummingbird; ☐ trapwire spider; ☐ tumble bug; ☐ walking stick; ☐ whirligig beetle; ☐ wolf spider; ☐ wood-boring beetle.

August

□ . . . .   □ . . . .   □ . . . .

□ . . . .   □ . . . .   □ . . . .

□ . . . .   □ . . . .   □ . . . .

□ . . . .   □ . . . .   □ . . . .

□ . . . .   □ . . . .   □ . . . .

WILDFLOWERS IN FIELDS AND MEADOWS:

□ bee balm; □ black-eyed Susan; □ blueberries; □ boneset; □ bouncing bet (soapwort); □ cranberries; □ fireweed; □ great blue lobelia; □ iron-weed; □ jewelweed; □ Joe-Pye weed; □ ladies' tresses; □ morning glories; □ pearly everlasting; □ raspberries; □ steeple blush; □ staghorn sumac; □ tansy; □ trumpet creeper; □ trumpet honeysuckle.

□ . . . .   □ . . . .   □ . . . .

□ . . . .   □ . . . .   □ . . . .

□ . . . .   □ . . . .   □ . . . .

. . . .

. . . .

. . . .

. . . .

. . . .

. . . .

. . . .

. . . .

. . . .

. . . .

. . . .

. . . .

Joe-Pye weed

August

....
....
....
....
....
....
....
....
....
....
....
....
....
....
....
....
....
....
....
....
....
....
....
....
....
....
....
....
....
....
....
....

September

*Before us lay a splendid world of sea
and shore. The autumn colors already
brightened the landscape; and here
and there at the edge of a dark tract
of pointed firs stood a row of bright
swamp-maples like scarlet flowers.
The blue sea and the great tide inlets
were untroubled by the lightest winds.*

SARAH ORNE JEWETT
Country of the Pointed Firs

September

TEETH AND QUILLS

And thus, without a Wing
Or service of a Keel
Our Summer made her light escape
Into the Beautiful.

EMILY DICKINSON

The Complete Poems of Emily Dickinson

In September the **woodchuck** (groundhog) fattens itself for winter hibernation with grasses, greens, and garden vegetables. When there's danger, the woodchuck grinds its teeth; other sounds include a loud whistle, a twittering chirp, and a chucking noise.

You may see one or more woodchucks sunning outside among their extensive dens. The dens are cleaned out several times a week, which is why there's a pile of earth in front. "Plunge holes" used to escape from enemies are dug from the inside so no telltale dirt shows. When winter comes, the woodchuck will plug the entrances, curl up in a ball, and go to sleep. A female's offspring (two to six in a litter) can reside in nearby tunnels all summer, but move far away to dig their own dens for winter.

Because of its eating habits, the **porcupine** is found only among spruce forests and Northern hardwoods, often returning to

porcupine

September

the same tree. It does most of its eating at night—bark and pine needles all year, tree buds in spring, nuts and fruit in summer, and salt, which it particularly craves. In winter hemlock branches on the snow probably mean that a porcupine is high above, nibbling tips and discarding the rest. You might hear the teeth-chattering sounds of the porcupine or a sniffing and meowing in the fall mating season.

Slow-moving with poor eyesight, this ten- to twenty-pound rodent protects itself by arching its back and raising the 30,000 barbed quills mixed in with its fur. A swat of the prickly tail drives off most attackers, and some loose quills may fly out and do even more damage. Like fur, quills are periodically shed and replaced.

NEAR THE WATER

Sometimes called "beaver's little brother," the **muskrat** also is brown, uses its powerful tail as a rudder, and has webbed hind feet. But a muskrat is no more than two feet long, and its ratlike tail is not as wide as a beaver's. In marshes, ponds, lakes, or streams it builds a small, mounded house made of reeds and cattails held together by mud. Water birds may nest on top. The muskrat is most active at night, eating aquatic plants on a feeding raft.

The frolicking **river otter** is a yard long, weasel-shaped, and has a stout tail. Several otters playfully wrestling along a river or lake bank look like seals with their glossy, streamlined bodies and sensitive whiskers, which help them find fish to eat in muddy water. Otter cubs are born all year and, surprisingly, have to be coaxed or pushed into water. It's not only babies that play. If you're lucky, you'll see cubs and adults bounding and sliding in the mud on their flat bellies. You may even see one juggling a pebble on its pointed nose.

Muskrat eat plants and otter eat fish. **Mink** devour fish, crayfish, and other mammals, especially young muskrats. This furry, chocolate brown, semiaquatic weasel the size of a cat is active mostly at night. Mother and father carry

September

babies by the scruff of the neck on land; in water, they give them a ride on their backs. Watch out for an excited mink—its musk smells worse than a skunk's.

INSECTS IN EARLY AUTUMN

How doth the little busy bee
Improve each shining hour,
And gather honey all the day,
From every opening flower.

ISAAC WATTS

"Song"

bumblebee

The bees that invariably appear when you're eating outside in the fall live in colonies, as ants do. "Social wasps" such as **yellow jackets** and **hornets** construct spacious, papery nests for their communities. You may find them under your eaves. Many solitary wasps nest singly in the ground; a solitary **mud dauber** makes a mud shelter for its eggs and provides each with its own insect or spider for food.

All summer worker bees have sucked nectar from flowers for honey to feed the adults and larvae in their colony. They also have gathered pollen on their hairy legs to make "bee bread" for the young. All along, they inadvertently have been fertilizing flowers with the pollen stuck to their bodies.

Sleepy, nonproductive drones are a drain on the colony once their job of fertilizing the queen is over. So in autumn, groups of workers bite, push, and drag drones out of the hive, leaving them to starve or be devoured by skunks, birds, and other insects. But the worker bee itself is not beyond threat of prey. Hiding in the **goldenrod** loaded with pollinating insects may be the tiny **ambush bug** with its huge "arms" and a "beak" which stabs and paralyzes prey larger than itself.

September

END OF SUMMER CHORUS

Male **cicadas** make that loud, incessant, mating buzz you hear using membranes on their abdomen. **Crickets** chirp and trill both night and day. **Katydids** call at night from trees and bushes by rubbing their front wings together. "Katy did," sings one group in unison. "Katy didn't," claims another.

> *Already, by the first of September, I had seen two or three small maples turned scarlet across the pond, beneath where the white stems of three aspens diverged, at the point of a promontory, next the water. Ah, many a tale their color told! And gradually from week to week the character of each tree came out, and it admired itself reflected in the smooth mirror of the lake. Each morning the manager of this gallery substituted some new picture, distinguished by more brilliant or harmonious coloring, for the old upon the walls.*
>
> HENRY DAVID THOREAU
> *Walden*

By now the climbing (false) **bittersweet** vine's yellow capsules have begun to split open to reveal showy scarlet berries. (True bittersweet is a nightshade, a different family.) Bittersweet berries "hang more gracefully over the river's edge than any pendant in a lady's ear," claims Thoreau in *Walden*.

A large orange rosehip has formed on the **rugosa** and other roses. **Mountain ash** berries are brilliant orange, **black alder** (winterberry) and **dogwood** berries are red, **Virginia creeper** blue, **baneberry** white, and **greenbriar** blue-black. Drooping, purple-black **pokeberries** make a crimson stain; purple-black **elderberries** attract forty-three kinds of bird species. Almost 100 birds eat wild **grapes**. Wild **plums** and **crabapples** (the only native apple tree) now are ripe; juicy wild **cherries** are devoured by song and

September

gamebirds, raccoon, bear, fox, deer, rabbit, and squirrel. **Pawpaws** have large, fleshy, green fruit and **persimmon** trees have cherrylike, orange ones. Colorful masses of goldenrod and **aster** blossoms are everywhere.

In the marsh **swamp maples** are scarlet, **bur reed** burs turn brown, and tall, majestic **phragmite** (common reed) plumes are silver buff. Look for **sedges** (unlike grasses, sedges have edges and solid rather than hollow stems.)

As cold weather withers and fades the last flowers, you're in for a treat if you can find in wet thickets and meadows the delicate **fringed blue gentian** and the intriguing, rich blue **closed** (bottle) **gentian**. A twittering in the bushes means **warblers** are migrating to the West Indies, Mexico, and South America. **Monarch butterflies** are on their way; watch for them on a sunny, salty headland.

> *The lands are lit*
> *With all the autumn blaze of Golden Rod;*
> *And everywhere the Purple Asters nod*
> *And bend and wave and flit.*
>
> HELEN HUNT
> *"Verses"*

CHECKLIST

WILDLIFE:

☐ ambush bug; ☐ bee; ☐ cicada; ☐ cricket;
☐ hornet; ☐ katydid; ☐ mink; ☐ monarch
butterfly; ☐ muskrat; ☐ mud dauber;
☐ porcupine; ☐ river otter; ☐ warbler;
☐ wasp; ☐ woodchuck; ☐ yellow jacket.
☐ . . . . ☐ . . . .
☐ . . . . ☐ . . . .
☐ . . . . ☐ . . . .

gentian

September

☐ aster; ☐ baneberry; ☐ bittersweet; ☐ black alder; ☐ bur reed;

☐ cherry; ☐ closed gentian; ☐ crabapple; ☐ dogwood; ☐ elderberry;

☐ fringed blue gentian; ☐ goldenrod; ☐ greenbriar; ☐ mountain ash;

☐ pawpaw; ☐ phragmite; ☐ pokeberry; ☐ rugosa; ☐ sedge; ☐ swamp
maple; ☐ Virginia creeper.

☐ . . . . ☐ . . . . ☐ . . . .

☐ . . . . ☐ . . . . ☐ . . . .

☐ . . . . ☐ . . . . ☐ . . . .

☐ . . . . ☐ . . . . ☐ . . . .

☐ . . . . ☐ . . . . ☐ . . . .

SOUTHWEST

More than anything else, the arid southwest to me means
sagebrush, the gray-green, usually low, bushy shrub which covers
many of the inter-mountain valleys from Colorado to California.
It encapsulates the history of the area, flourishing where over-
grazing by sheep and cattle has killed out the native grasses.
Antelope and grouse, mule deer and elk count it an important part
of their diet, so it helps to keep alive the wildness, which I hope
will never disappear entirely from this region...The tiny, three-
toothed leaves of sagebrush (its botanical name is artemisia
tridentata) instantly stimulates intense memories of my childhood:
hiking across shallow basins into the arroyos reaching out from
bony ridges of hills...horizontal rays of golden, afternoon sunlight
transforming every familiar color into a more vivid palette...desert
rain, those first pelting drops stirring up the very body-scent of
aridity from dusk and rock and resinous foliage.

PATRICIA M. FOWLER

September

WILDLIFE:

☐ armadillo; ☐ cactus wren; ☐ chuckwalla; ☐ coyote; ☐ deer; ☐ eagle; ☐ gila monster; ☐ gilded flicker; ☐ Harris hawk; ☐ horned lizard; ☐ hummingbird; ☐ jack rabbit; ☐ kangaroo rat; ☐ peccary; ☐ prairie dog; ☐ red-tail hawk; ☐ road runner; ☐ topknot quail; ☐ wild turkey.

PLANT LIFE:

☐ cacti; ☐ desert marigold; ☐ flannel flower; ☐ four o'clock; ☐ golden star; ☐ greasewood; ☐ groundsel; ☐ mesquite; ☐ paloverde; ☐ prickly poppy; ☐ sagebrush; ☐ sand verbena; ☐ tidy-top; ☐ yucca.

. . . .
. . . .
. . . .
. . . .
. . . .
. . . .
. . . .
. . . .
. . . .
. . . .
. . . .
. . . .
. . . .
. . . .
. . . .
. . . .
. . . .
. . . .

September

prickly pear

 September

October

The morns are meeker than they were,
The nuts are getting brown;
The berry's cheek is plumper,
The rose is out of town.

The maple wears a gayer scarf,
The field a scarlet gown,
Lest I should be old-fashioned,
I'll put a trinket on.

EMILY DICKINSON
Autumn

October

FALL CHANGES

As the days grow shorter and the nights colder, as the sun arcs lower and a harvest moon rises orange in the autumn sky, **false Solomon's seal** berries turn translucent ruby-red, **ferns** are golden, and **blueberry** and **sumac** leaves scarlet. Silky **milkweed** parachutes drift in the wind; **pines** are shedding; crinkled, fragrant **osage orange** fruits are the size of grapefruit; **bur reeds** lie limp in the marshes, and the damp smell of leaf mold hovers in the air.

Chipmunks chip persistently, but insect sounds become slower and more drawn out. **Red-wing blackbirds** are restless, and flocks of **blue jays** and **robins** arrive from the North. On moonlit nights thousands of **hawks**, songbirds, shorebirds, and **Canada geese** migrate south. Snakes soak up the sun; bats have vanished. The tails of squirrels and the pelts of foxes, skunks, and raccoons thicken. Squirrels and chipmunks store industriously for winter; moles dig below the frost line, and beavers insulate their lodges with sturdy new sticks and mud.

But the truly spectacular seasonal change is the tree color of fall—the crimson and vivid yellow of **maples**, the gold of **hickories**, the wine red of **tupelos**, the bronze, russet, and cinnamon of **oaks.**

Fall's lustrous display of colors is the product of adaptation and survival. The shorter days of autumn trigger in trees the instinct to protect themselves from the coming cold by forming an extra cell layer. This layer cuts off production of the chlorophyll that makes leaves green. As a result, the other colors already present in leaves can emerge—the yellow xanthophyll and red and orange carotene pigments, along with blends of these, produce the splendid color mosaic of fall leaves.

When the leaves have fallen, startled **grouse** noisily take wing in the dry woods. Bird, squirrel, and hornet nests are more visible in the forest skeleton, and tree trunks sway and bend in the autumn gusts.

October

SQUIRRELS

"Squirrel" comes from the Greek, "skiourus," he who sits in the shadow of his tail. The squirrel uses this essential appendage for balance, for warmth, and as a parachute when descending from high places.

Gray squirrels collect and bury hundreds of nuts and fruits. Later, when hungry, they will smell them out even under the snow. In spring a squirrel may "tap" a sugar maple and lap the sweet syrup. Winter living quarters is a den built as high as sixty feet in a tree hole or leaf nest. The base of twigs of this nest or "drey" was probably first constructed by a large bird. The squirrels give it a domed roof.

squirrel

Males will become more aggressive with each other in December and January and chase females throughout the trees. Babies are born forty-four days after mating and take two years to be grown, so the previous litter will stay in the den all winter.

Red squirrels are found in the evergreens of the North—scolding, barking, stamping feet, and flicking tails. Food supplies are not buried one-by-one, but stored in burrows or under fallen trees or roots. Discarded nutshells and cone scales can build to a large pile (midden). Spruce and pine cones are harvested when still green; mushrooms are put on branches to cure, then tucked under loose bark.

The large, slow, and late-rising **fox squirrels** live in the East, except New England. They spend more time on the ground than their daring relatives, the **flying squirrels**, which hole up in dead trees during the day and in cold, wet weather. At night flying squirrels spread their limbs and glide from branch

October

to ground, with the loose skin that joins the front legs to hind legs and tail acting as a stabilizer.

The West's **Douglas squirrel** is "the mockingbird of squirrels, pouring forth chatter and song like a perennial fountain; barking like a dog, screaming like a hawk, chirping like a blackbird or sparrow; while in bluff audacious noisiness he is a very jay," according to John Muir in *Wild Animals of North America*.

BEARS

By now furry **black bears** have begun their winter snooze. Fattened by berries, roots, bark, grass, ants, rodents, bees, and honey, the male and female will stay in their separate dens in caves or hollow trees until spring, unless a warm spell lures them outside. Twin cubs are born in midwinter. Bears mark trees with their claws and teeth. Ernest Thompson Seton called them "signboards" for other bears. Stretching exercises is offered as another theory.

MIGRATING HAWKS

Hawks get help in their migration when a high pressure area moves down from the Arctic bringing cold weather, wind, and clear sky. Hawks glide southward on the updrafts along particular mountain ridges. One autumn day observers counted 211,448 over Hawk Mountain Sanctuary in Pennsylvania.

red-tailed hawk

By October, **broad-winged hawks** (a crow-sized buteo with a broadly banded tail) are well on their way from the Florida Keys to winter homes in Brazil. **Red-tails** (with a rufous upper tail and dark belly-band) winter on the Gulf Coast and in northern Nicaragua. **Swainson's hawks** (a dark-breasted, western buteo) fly the farthest—to northern Argentina.

October

Hawks may soar 1,000 feet or more, but a **vulture** actually holds the altitude record. In 1921 a British expedition on Mount Everest spotted one 25,000 feet high.

Nuts

> *And, close at hand, the basket stood*
> *With nuts from brown October's wood.*
>
> John Greenleaf Whittier
> *Snowbound*

Pollinated nut tree flowers become fruit—a husk which protects a nutmeat inside a shell. The **oak**'s familiar acorns are eaten by many herbivorous birds and mammals. Edible too are the fruit of sweet hickories. **Shagbark hickories** are found in uplands, **shellbark** in lowlands; both have pale gray strips of curling bark.

Tall, spreading **pecans** are a southern and lower Mississippi Valley relative of the hickory. Their bark is light brown-gray, rough, and broken. **Butternuts** are a cold-resistant walnut tree whose oblong fruits are covered with sticky hairs.

Lofty **black walnuts** have dark brown, deeply furrowed bark and spicy smelling, paired leaves which shed early. The fruit's husk is green at first, then black and rotten-looking.

Beechnut bark is a smooth gray, and the pale leaves hang on into the winter. Nuts are small and triangular and don't come every year. Beeches grow in deep woods. Look for shrublike **hazelnuts** in pastures, wood edges, or forest clearings. The fruit husks may be flared or tubular.

Ground nuts are not a nut from a tree but "Indian potatoes" on a vine. Tubers are underground, "strung along the roots like round pearls in a necklace," says naturalist Edwin Way Teale.

October

WILDLIFE CHECKLIST

□ black bear; □ chipmunks; □ Douglas squirrel; □ fox squirrel; □ flying squirrel; □ gray squirrel; □ red squirrel.

□ .... □ .... □ ....

□ .... □ .... □ ....

HAWKS AND OTHER BIRDS:

□ broad-winged hawk; □ Canada geese; □ red-tail hawk; □ red-wing; □ robin; □ Swainson's hawk; □ vulture.

□ .... □ .... □ ....

□ .... □ .... □ ....

NUTS, TREES, LEAVES AND FALL VEGETATION:

□ beechnuts; □ black walnuts; □ bur reeds; □ butternuts; □ ferns; □ ground nuts; □ hazelnuts; □ hickories; □ maples; □ milkweed; □ oak; □ osage orange; □ pecans; □ pines; □ shagbark hickories; □ shellbark; □ sumac; □ tupelo.

□ .... □ .... □ ....

□ .... □ .... □ ....

□ .... □ ....

□ .... □ ....

□ .... □ ......

□ .... □ ......

□ .... □ ....

□ .... □ ....

□ ....

□ ....

□ ....

□ ....

nuts and leaves

October

October

November

Dry leaves upon the wall,
Which flap like rustling wings and seek
escape,
A single frosted cluster on the grape
Still hangs — and that is all.

SUSAN COOLIDGE
"A Nip in the Air"

November

DUCKS

The migrating ducks of North America follow four ancient flyways on their way from frozen breeding grounds to winter feeding places: the Atlantic, the Mississippi, the Central, and the Pacific. Starting out in late afternoon, they fly through the night, guided by the stars on clear days. For waterfowl, weather conditions are crucial: fog can ground them; snow, torrential rain, and hail can kill them.

River and **pond ducks** are surface feeders that dabble—head tipped, tail up—in shallow water for aquatic plants and seeds. **Bay ducks** dive deeply and swim for plants, insects, and mollusks. Under water they hold their small, pointed wings tight against their body to keep dry.

Both river and bay ducks move their webbed feet alternately as paddles; on the backstroke, toes and webs are closed for less resistance. Their salt glands eliminate salt from the water they drink. A network of arteries and veins keep duck feet from freezing in icy weather.

During the day, **black ducks** gather to form large rafts in open water. At night they feed in salt marshes, ponds, and mudflats. **Mallards** prefer swamps, streams, and rice fields in the Gulf states, lower Mississippi valley, and west into Texas, but hardy individuals will winter in the North wherever there's open water.

Riding the waves in huge rafts of up to 50,000, bay ducks are the **eider**, **scaup**, and **scoter**. Eider flocks follow curving coastlines and detour around headlands to avoid land and stay over water.

SWANS

Tundra (whistling) **swans** don't whistle. One writer describes their call as "soft trumpeting like musical laughter." Flying together with powerful wingbeats and with graceful necks extended, they spread ribbonlike across the sky. Pure white, tundra swans resemble the **mute swans** (Eurasian

November

imports) except for their black (not orange) beak and erect (not curved) neck. Like dabbling ducks, swans tip to feed. They mate for life and migrate above the clouds as they return from Arctic breeding grounds. Half of their entire population returns in the fall to the Chesapeake Bay, stopping along the way on the Great Lakes.

The "swan song" of legend turns out to be true. Several naturalists report that when shot, the "departure song" of a tundra swan plummeting to earth is plaintive, melodious, and haunting.

GEESE

Autumn weather on our bird farm in the rolling Berkshires of Connecticut brings crisp evenings, the early reddening of the maples, and a sense of restless movement in the air...skeins of Canada geese appear early each evening—fifteen or more flying low. But most of the geese are higher, often in much larger groups, their ululations ringing wildly, echoing through the hills. Sometimes in the deeper blue haze long after sunset, we cannot really see them, but only hear the wild calls that trail away faintly, stirring the blood, evoking thoughts of times long past, of other days and distant places on the land.

S. DILLON RIPLEY
The American Land

Canada geese migrate by day at forty to sixty miles per hour in V formations and strung-out lines. Flight leaders spell each other along the way. Each goose, by flying close behind another, takes

tundra swan

November

advantage of the slip-stream or drafting effect of the wing-tips, saving energy. If positioned directly behind, however, the disturbed air can throw the goose off track, so it stays just to the side.

After sunrise and before sunset, in corn fields or marshes, sentinels watch and warn of danger with a display of head tossing and guttural sounds. Before taking off, Canada geese face the wind and run a few steps with wings furiously beating. When landing, they thrust feet forward, toes spread. Most Canada geese breed in the Arctic or sub-Arctic, and winter throughout the United States, especially on the Chesapeake Bay and along coastal North Carolina. Pairs mate for life, and families stay together throughout fall and winter.

Arctic **snow geese** have pure white plumage. Yet their scientific name, *Anser caerulescens*, means bluish, referring to a phase of the smaller variant, the **lesser snow geese** (blue geese), with slate-gray feathers. Snow geese fly almost nonstop from the Arctic to Louisiana coastal marshes.

Maritime **brant geese** travel in tight clusters that shift to wavy lines; they rest on sandbars and, like eider ducks, have an aversion to crossing low over land. In the 1930s, the survival of brant geese was threatened when their principal food, eelgrass, was nearly destroyed in a blight. Enough brant geese, however, averted disaster by adapting and learning to eat algae, sea cabbage, and sea lettuce instead.

ruffled grouse

GAMEBIRDS

When startled, **ruffled grouse** spring into the air with a whir that's magnified in the dry-leaved, quiet woods.

November

In the fall **pheasants** grow a comblike projection beside their toes to help them walk on top of the snow. On winter nights they dive and tunnel under the snow for warmth. Unlike the grouse, the pheasant—an immigrant from China—prefers open country, and when flushed, often runs rather than flies to safety.

Belying its chunky body, the **bobwhite** is a swift riser and rapid runner when seeking cover. At night they roost in a circle under shrub cover, with tails huddled in the center and heads out, each bird lifting its wings slightly to spread warmth.

In 1831, Audubon wrote that he'd seen **wild turkeys** roll in an ants' nest "to clear their growing feathers of the loose scales and prevent ticks and other vermin from attacking them, these insects being unable to bear the odor of the earth in which ants have been." Since then, naturalists have estimated some 200 birds practice "anting" as a form of feather maintenance. They believe the ants squirt out formic acid, which acts as an insecticide killing parasites.

MOSS AND LICHEN

Throughout the fall, even after the leaves have gone, mosses and lichen color the woods. Lichen is actually two plants, an alga and a fungus in symbiosis. The alga has chlorophyll and through photosynthesis provides food for both; fungus breaks down the decaying logs and other matter on which the lichen need to grow.

Hair-cap moss grows in soft patches; spore capsules are on spikes. Pluck off the tan hood of the hair capsule, then pry up the cap of the "cookie jar" underneath. Inside are yellow and green, pollenlike spores, "used by elfmen to paint the woods," this author was told as a child. **Pixie cup** lichen are miniature, brown cups the size of a drop of dew; **reindeer** lichen are gray and grow in patches and branches like antlers.

November

Checklist

LICHEN:

☐ British soldier; ☐ conch; ☐ pink earth; ☐ pixie cup; ☐ reindeer.

☐ . . . . ☐ . . . . ☐ . . . .

MOSSES:

☐ hair-cap; ☐ sphagnum; ☐ pincushion.

☐ . . . . ☐ . . . . ☐ . . . .

RIVER AND POND DUCKS:

☐ baldpate; ☐ black duck; ☐ blue-winged teal; ☐ green-winged teal;
☐ mallard; ☐ pintail; ☐ shoveler; ☐ wood duck.

☐ . . . . ☐ . . . . ☐ . . . .
☐ . . . . ☐ . . . . ☐ . . . .

BAY DUCKS:

☐ American merganser; ☐ bufflehead; ☐ canvasback; ☐ eider; ☐ golden-
eye; ☐ oldsquaw; ☐ ring-neck; ☐ scaup; ☐ scoter.

☐ . . . . ☐ . . . . ☐ . . . .
☐ . . . . ☐ . . . . ☐ . . . .

GEESE:

☐ brant goose; ☐ Canada goose; ☐ lesser snow goose; ☐ snow goose.

☐ . . . . ☐ . . . . ☐ . . . .

SWANS:

☐ mute swan; ☐ tundra swan.

☐ . . . . ☐ . . . . ☐ . . . .

GAMEBIRDS:

☐ bobwhite; ☐ pheasant; ☐ ruffled grouse; ☐ wild turkey.

☐ . . . . ☐ . . . . ☐ . . . .

November

wood duck

November

December

The snow had begun in the gloaming,
  And busily all the night
Had been heaping field and highway
  With a silence deep and white.

  Every pine and fir and hemlock
  Wore ermine too dear for an earl,
And the poorest twig on the elm-tree
  Was ridged inch deep with pearl.

JAMES RUSSELL LOWELL
"The First Snow-Fall"

December

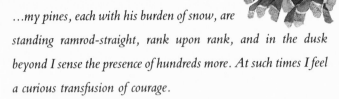

LIFE IN THE DEAD OF WINTER

*...my pines, each with his burden of snow, are
standing ramrod-straight, rank upon rank, and in the dusk
beyond I sense the presence of hundreds more. At such times I feel
a curious transfusion of courage.*

ALDO LEOPOLD

A Sand County Almanac

Recognizing one evergreen from another means knowing its needles. **Pine** trees have bundles of long, thin needles that shed. **Hemlock** needles are flat with a tiny stem. **Balsam** needles also are flat, but have no stem, and give off a pleasant smell when crushed. **Spruce** needles are four-sided and sharp. They hold the snow and offer animals good shelter from the wind. The beautiful **American larch** (called tamarack in some places, hackmatack in others) turns golden in the fall and sheds all of its slender needles.

Of the evergreen ferns, **Christmas ferns** are the largest. They're dark green in the snow and resemble indoor Boston ferns. **Woodferns** grow in swampy lowlands and woods and already show next year's fiddleheads (some consider them delicacies when cooked).

Club mosses cluster in small colonies and look like miniature evergreen trees. A form of fern which grew 300 million years ago, club mosses then were large trees. They became a source of fossil fuel; coal has been made from their roots, stems, and leaves.

The "thief tree" is an appropriate name for **mistletoe,** which actually is a partial parasite growing on host trees. Found largely in the Mid-Atlantic and the South, especially in the Gulf states, mistletoe's berries are poisonous if eaten. In the Middle Ages they were hung from ceilings to ward off evil spirits; now we hang them in holiday celebration. Also in the Mid-Atlantic and South, look for **greenbriar** and **holly**. **Beetlewood** has dark, heart-shaped

December

leaves and grows in the southern Appalachians.

The stalks and seed cases of the tiny **pipsissewa** rise above the snow under northern pines and oaks. **Juniper**, a shrub with gray-blue berries, lives in old fields and on mountain slopes, along with **rhododendron** and **laurel**. The dry flower parts of the laurel are visible; leaves are dark and shiny. Rhododendron leaves curl up in winter.

American holly

The thin snow now driving from the north and lodging on my coat consists of those beautiful star crystals, not cottony and chubby spokes as on the 13th of December, but thin and partly transparent crystals. They are about one-tenth of an inch in diameter, perfect little wheels with six spokes....

What a world we live in, where myriads of these little disks, so beautiful to the most prying eye, are whirled down on every traveler's coat, the observant and the unobservant, on the restless squirrel's fur, on the far-stretching fields and forests, the wooded dells and the mountain tops. Far, far from the haunts of men. They roll down some little slope, fall over and come to their bearings, and melt or lose their beauty in the mass, ready anon to swell some little rill with their contribution, and so at last the universal ocean from which they came.

HENRY DAVID THOREAU
Walden and Other Writings

December

Cranberry is found in bogs and rocky areas. **Teaberry**, a member of the heath family, grows in the woods, its red berries hidden by bright, green leaves. **Partridge berry** thrives under white pine. Its berries also are red, but the leaves are dark green with veins. The bright green leaves of the **trailing arbutus** can be seen growing in rocky or sandy places.

Galls are growths on leaves and trees made by insects for protection. They are seen on oak trees, spruces (pineapple shaped), goldenrod (round and elliptical) and willows (pine-cone shaped and petaled). Inside the growth is the insect that made the gall.

Hidden under the bark of trees are hibernating beetles and spiders, insect pupae, and egg cases—all sought by birds as food. On the outer bark of dead trees are "engravings" carved by bark beetles or "galleries" burrowed out and chewed by carpenter ants.

Bracket fungi are semicircular, with the consistency of leather, and grow in clusters on both dead and live tree trunks. These plants have no chlorophyll, so they must feed from other plants. Each bracket begins with a spore in the bark from which threadlike strands collect nutrition. The growth pushed outside the tree will produce more spores; beneath seemingly lifeless fungi are billions of spores.

ON REFLECTION

How lonely are my days? How solitary are my nights?....by the mountains of snow which surround me I could almost fancy myself in Greenland. We have had four of the coldest days I ever knew, and they were followed by the severest snowstorm I ever remember, the wind blowing like a hurricane for 15 or 20 hours rendered it almost impossible for man or beast to live abroad, and has blocked up the roads so that they are impassable.

ABIGAIL ADAMS TO JOHN, *December 27, 1778*

December

And yet, on the coldest, dreariest winter day, there can be found signs of spring. Look—just above the round or oblong stem scars left on tree twigs by the fallen leaves of fall are scale-covered buds. Tucked securely within them are the new leaves of spring.

> *The image of the wintering tree as a symbol of death and emptiness must itself die, for in reality, winter trees already contain the coming year's leaves and flowers.*
>
> DONALD W. STOKES
>
> *A Guide to Nature in Winter*

larch

CHECKLIST

EVERGREENS AND PLANTS:

☐ American larch; ☐ balsam; ☐ beetlewood; ☐ bracket fungus; ☐ Christmas fern; ☐ club moss; ☐ cranberry; ☐ gall; ☐ greenbriar; ☐ hemlock; ☐ holly; ☐ juniper; ☐ laurel; ☐ mistletoe; ☐ partridge berry; ☐ pine; ☐ pipsissewa; ☐ rhododendron ☐ spruce; ☐ teaberry; ☐ trailing arbutus; ☐ winterberry; ☐ woodfern.

☐ . . . .   ☐ . . . .   ☐ . . . .
☐ . . . .   ☐ . . . .   ☐ . . . .
☐ . . . .   ☐ . . . .   ☐ . . . .
☐ . . . .   ☐ . . . .   ☐ . . . .
☐ . . . .   ☐ . . . .   ☐ . . . .

. . . .
. . . .
. . . .

December

Pacific Coast Wildlife

I've counted 90 kinds of wildflowers on the headlands over the ocean. In the early spring are field mustard, wild radish, periwinkle, scarlet pimpernel, California rockcress, milkmaids, footprints of spring, scarlet columbine to name a few. The lupine is beautiful—purple, yellow and white. Later we have penny royal, Douglas iris, mule ears, millions of sunflowers, roses, sticky cinquefoil—onion-type flowers. Then it gets dry in the summer, and by September the flowers are gone.

WILLIAM E. EATON

Checklist

Wildlife unique to the coast are found at Point Reyes and Farallon Islands National Marine Sanctuary, at Muir Woods and at Yosemite National Park, including:

☐ black-tailed deer; ☐ California Bay laurel; ☐ California gull; ☐ California quail; ☐ California thrasher; ☐ chickadee; ☐ elephant seal; ☐ gray whale; ☐ mule deer; ☐ murres; ☐ Oregon junco; ☐ petrel; ☐ pigmy owl; ☐ pinyon jay; ☐ puffin; ☐ redwood; ☐ scrub jay; ☐ sea lion; ☐ sea otter; ☐ sequoia; ☐ Sonoma chipmunk; ☐ Steller's jay; ☐ Steller's sea lion.

☐ . . . . ☐ . . . . ☐ . . . .

☐ . . . . ☐ . . . . ☐ . . . .

☐ . . . . ☐ . . . . ☐ . . . .

☐ . . . . ☐ . . . . ☐ . . . .

. . . .

. . . .

. . . .

. . . .

. . . .

December

We began to climb without much talk among bushy pines where congenial pinon jays flickered. Suddenly we halted, all of us, in a clearing; purple lupine in full bloom grew so thickly that we could not find our path. I stopped just as the sun flooded this world with brilliance, concentrated and sparkling in dewdrops clustered on each of the knee-high blossoms which surrounded me. The center of the universe could be seen in each globule, with straw-gold light and birdsong rippling outward. I was eternally tied to it all, as though I was not even there.

PATRICIA K. FOWLER

lupine

BIBLIOGRAPHY

PERMISSIONS

The author is grateful for the permission of the following publishers and authors to quote copyrighted material from the following works:

Carson, Rachel. *The Edge of the Sea.* Copyright © 1955 by Rachel I. Carson. Reprinted by permission of Houghton Mifflin Company.

Leopold, Aldo. *A Sand County Almanac.* Copyright © 1949. Reprinted by permission of Oxford University Press.

Peterson, Roger Tory. *Gardening With Wildlife.* Copyright © 1974. Reprinted by permission of National Wildlife Federation.

Richmond, Chandler S. *Beyond the Spring: Cordelia Stanwood of Birdsacre.* Copyright © 1978. Reprinted by permission of the author.

Ripley, S. Dillon. *The American Land.* Copyright © 1979. Reprinted by permission of Smithsonian Books.

Stevens, Wallace. "Thirteen Ways of Looking at a Blackbird," *Harmonium.* Copyright © 1923, 1931. Reprinted by permission of Alfred A. Knopf.

Stokes, Donald W. *A Guide to Nature in Winter: Northeast and Central America.* Copyright © 1976. Reprinted by permission of Little, Brown.

Teale, Edwin Way. *A Walk Through the Year.* Copyright © 1978. Reprinted by permission of Dodd, Mead & Company, Inc.

BOOKS

Angell, Madeline. *America's Best Loved Wild Animals.* Indianapolis and New York, 1975.

Audubon Society. *The Audubon Society Field Guide of North American Wildflowers.* New York, 1979.

Audubon Society & Bull, John. *The Audubon Society Guide of North American Birds.* New York, 1977.

Borland, Hal. *The History of Wildlife in America.* Washington, D.C., 1975.

Brown, Lauren. *Weeds in Winter.* Boston, 1977.

Carson, Rachel. *The Edge of the Sea.* Boston, 1955.

Clement, Roland C. *Hammond Nature Atlas of America.* Maplewood, New York, 197?.

Durrell, Gerald & Durrell, Lee. *The Amateur Naturalist.* New York, 1983.

Grehan, Farrell & Rickett, H. W. *The Golden Book of American Wildflowers.* New York, 1964.

Kartright, Francis H. *The Ducks, Geese and Swans of North America.* Harrisburg, Pennsylvania, 1967.

Leopold, Aldo. *A Sand County Almanac & Sketches Here and There.* London, 1949.

Mitchell, John H. *A Field Guide to Your Own Back Yard.* New York, 1985.

Murphy, Robert. *Wild Sanctuaries.* New York, 1968.

National Geographic Society. *Wondrous World of Fishes.* Washington, D.C., 1965.

National Wildlife Federation. *Gardening With Wildlife.* Washington, D.C., 1974.

Nowak, Ronald, et al. Allen, Thomas B., Ed. *Wild Animals of North America.* Washington, D.C., 1960.

Peterson, Roger Tory. *A Field Guide to the Birds.* Boston, 1959.

Petrides, George A. *Field Guide to Trees and Shrubs.* Boston, 1972.

Porter, Eliot. *"In the Wilderness Is the Preservation of the World."* San Francisco, 1962.

Reader's Digest Editors. *America From the Road: A Motorist's Guide to Our Country's Natural Wonders and Most Interesting Places.* New York, 1982.

Richmond, Chandler S. *Beyond the Spring: Cordelia Stanwood of Birdsacre.* Lamoine, Maine, 1978.

Robins, Chandler S., et al. *Birds of North America.* New York, 1966.

Smithsonian Institution. *The American Land: The Smithsonian Book of the American Environment.* (A Smithsonian Exposition Book.) Washington, D.C., 1979.

Steven, David, Ed. *Encyclopedia of Animals.* New York, 1965.

Stokes, Donald W. *A Guide to Nature in Winter: Northeast and North Central North America.* Boston, 1976.

Teal, Edwin W. *A Walk Through the Year.* New York, 1978.

Terres, John K. *The Audubon Society Encyclopedia of North American Birds.* New York, 1980.

Wetmore, Alexander. *Water, Prey, and Game Birds of North America.* Washington, D.C., 1965.

Song and Garden Birds of North America. Washington, D.C., 1964.

MAGAZINES

Fergus, Charles. "Wild Nuts: A Gatherer's Compendium." *Country Journal,* 11/84.

Rupp, Rebecca. "Squirrels." *Country Journal,* 10/84.

Ryden, Hope. "The White-Tailed Deer." *Country Journal,* 11/84.

Yurus, John. "The River Otter." *Country Journal,* 1/86.

INDEX

Note: Checklist items are not indexed unless discussed in the text.

INDEX

INDEX